Citizenship Studies

C000175751

for AQA GCSE Short Course

**Mike Mitchell, Dave Jones
and David Worden**

Hodder Murray

A MEMBER OF THE HODDER HEADLINE GROUP

Dedicated to Charlotte, in the hope that she and her generation gain from their study of Citizenship.

Acknowledgements

The publishers would like to thank the following individuals, institutions and companies for permission to reproduce copyright illustrations in this book:

AP Photos: p112 (tl) Achmad Ibrahim, (r) Moshe Bursuker, p90 Ruth Fremson; p13 Jacqueline Burden; BBC Picture Archives: p72; ChildLine: p72; Neil Cooper Pictures: p75; Corbis: p7 Raymond Gehman, p8, p88 Bettman/Corbis, p92 Francoise de Mulder; p12 Richard T Nowitz, p81 (l) Chris Rainier; p14 Roger Ressmeyer, p16 Flip Schulke, p21 Robert & Linda Mostyn/Eye Ubiquitous, p24 (t) Ian Harwood/Ecoscene, (m) Owen Franken, (b) Robert Holmes, p26 Nik Wheeler, p28 (r) So Hing-Keung, p44 (m) Najlah Feanny, p44 (2r) Craig Aurness, p47, p83 David Turnley, p52 John Heseltine, p81 Robert Holmes, p101 Vittoriano Rastelli, p103, p107 Peter Johnson, p104 Robert Maass, p106 Owen Franken, p108 Joe Bator, p112 (bl) Michael S Yamashita; Council of Europe: p44 (l), p56; Express Newspapers p66 (far right); Melanie Friend/Format: p97; Foto Web UPPA Ltd: p70 (r); James Hawkins/Oxfam: p94; Hulton Archive: p86 Hulton Getty/Fox Photos; ITN: p72 (br); Life File: p38 (l) Mike Evans; Mirror Syndication: p66; PA News: p38 (r) Martin Keane; News International Syndication: p66 (far left), p68 (l) and (br); PA Photos: p39, p60 (l); p9, p42 (m), 44 (r), 67, 80, 91, 97, 100, 101, 126 EPA, p27 Owen Humphreys, p28 (l) Sean Dempsey, p33 David Cheskin, p40 Dave Kendall, p44 (2l) Fiona Hanson, p42 Barry Batchelor, p51 Phil Noble, p60 (r) Matthew Fearn, p61, p72(br) John Giles, p63 Justin Williams, p65 Peter Jordan, p42 (r), pp 42 (r), 68 (t) Toby Melville, p71 Yui Mok, p76 Stefan Rousseau, p89 Paul Faith, p98 Andy Butterton; Photodisk: p22; Photofusion: p6 David Tothill, p11 Gina Glover, p15 G Montgomery, p29, p32 Paul Doyle, p30, p46 Brian Mitchell, p34 Peter Olive, p35 Don Gray, p48 Ute Klaphake, p77 Mark Campbell, p95 Paul Bigland, p109; Reuters/Popperfoto: p66 (2r); Rex Features Ltd: p31 Ray Tang, pp37, 73 Nils Jorgensen, p41 Tony Kyriacou, p70 (l) Dan Herrick, p88 (l) Sipa Press; Ronald Grant Archive: p72; Shelter: p37 (r); Steven Lawrence Trust: p62 photo reproduced by kind permission of Doreen Lawrence, Director of the Stephen Lawrence Trust; Still Pictures: p96, p98 (r) Hartmut Schwarzbach; Topham/Picturepoint: p105.

The publishers would also like to thank the following for permission to reproduce material in this book:

A message from the HM Queen Elizabeth 11 March 2002 – cleared personally by Her Majesty, via the Lord Chamberlain's Office. Reproduced with the permission of the Controller of HMSO; p36 The Citizenship Foundation ; p26 quote from The Guardian © Matt Weaver. This material first appeared in The Guardian 26 July 2002; Common Courage Press for extracts from *Eyes of the Heart; Seeking Poor in the Age of Globalisation* by Jean-Bertrand Aristide.

Orders: please contact Bookpoint Ltd, 130 Milton Park, Abingdon, Oxon OX14 4SB. Telephone: (44) 01235 827720. Fax: (44) 01235 400454. Lines are open from 9.00–6.00, Monday to Saturday, with a 24 hour message answering service. You can also order through our website www.hoddereducation.co.uk

British Library Cataloguing in Publication Data
A catalogue record for this title is available from the British Library

ISBN 10: 0 340 85044 2
ISBN 13: 978 0 340 85044 2

First Published 2002
Impression number   10 9 8 7 6 5 4
Year   2007 2006 2005

Copyright © 2002 Dave Jones, Mike Mitchell and David Worden.

All rights reserved. No part of this publication may be reproduced or transmitted in any form or by any means, electronic or mechanical, including photocopy, recording, or any information storage and retrieval system, without permission in writing from the publisher or under licence from the Copyright Licensing Agency Limited. Further details of such licences (for reprographic reproduction) may be obtained from the Copyright Licensing Agency Limited, of 90 Tottenham Court Road, London W1T 4LP.

Cover photo from Digital Vision.
Typeset by Pantek Arts, Maidstone, Kent.
Printed in Italy for Hodder Murray, an imprint of Hodder Education, a member of the Hodder Headline Group, 338 Euston Road, London NW1 3BH.

Contents

KEY ISSUES

- ○ What qualities help to make a person a good citizen?
- ○ How do we make the right choices and decisions?
- ○ How might our choices and decisions affect others?

Choices and Decisions

'Citizenship education is education for citizenship, behaving and acting as a citizen. Therefore it is not just knowledge of citizenship and civil society, it also implies developing values, skills and understanding.'

The Crick Report, paragraph 3:1, 1998.

This means that Citizenship education is aimed not only at supplying knowledge and understanding of how society works, but also at providing the skills that enable young people to take part in society as active citizens of our democracy. Citizenship is about fairness, democracy, justice, rights, responsibilities, participation and choice, and this book looks at how citizenship is developed through the following topics:

1 School, Work and the Local Community.
2 National and European Citizenship.
3 Global Citizenship.

Citizens need to find out the facts, consider the alternatives, weigh up the consequences, make their decision and then take action. Citizenship involves learning from the outcomes of the choices and decisions we have taken. It may mean being actively involved in campaigning for a fairer society.

Deciding what is the right choice or decision to make is not always easy. What we decide usually has an impact on other people as well. Our actions affect others – we are citizens of the local, national and international communities. The decisions we make have an effect on ourselves, our family and friends, our community and the world. We all have rights, but we also have responsibilities, and trying to work out what is the best or right course of action in a particular situation can be difficult.

How Do You Decide What is Right and What is Wrong?

Many things influence us when we make our choices. These include:

- Considering the consequences of our actions.
- Rules and regulations (e.g. the law or school rules).
- Our feelings and beliefs (e.g. is it morally right? Believers consider their religious beliefs).
- Our parents and peers.
- Our own experiences and knowledge.

Shane needs a new pair of trainers for school. He realises that there are many decisions and choices that he is able to make. What should he take into consideration if he is to make an informed choice?

Some of the issues include:

- What size, style, colour and make should he choose?
- How much should he pay?
- Does he need to look cool and buy a brand that his classmates would approve of?
- Does his image really matter?
- Should he consider wider issues such as the conditions under which the trainers were produced and whether or not they are **eco-friendly**?
- Could some cheap trainers be shoddy or counterfeit or genuine bargains?
- What about their comfort, reliability and durability?

Shane knows that most of his **peer** group (friends) wear a particular brand of trainers, which are regarded as cool. He has heard that the company that produces them has had a lot of criticism in the past for using child labour and for the working conditions of their employees. They were accused of allowing toxic fumes into their factories and of not taking adequate safety precautions to protect their employees. It was claimed that wages were so low that workers had to do excessive overtime in order to obtain enough money to have a living wage. Allegations included a claim that it was extremely difficult to obtain sick leave and that the annual leave was often refused. Workers who complained

Should Shane be pushed into buying a particular brand of trainers because of what his mates would say? Should he make a stand as a matter of principle and try to influence his friends? What action could be taken which might help to influence a company that was accused of treating their workers unfairly?

Living in a Global Economy
An example of how the system works:

1 Origin of the idea in a multinational company.
2 Finance obtained for setting up the enterprise (e.g. borrowed from American banks).
3 Design of the trainers (e.g. in Germany).
4 Building of factories/employment of labour (e.g. Pakistan and Thailand).
5 Production line controlled by computers made in South Korea.
6 Hong Kong shipping line employed to transport trainers to the markets.
7 Italian company employed to design the publicity/advertisements.
8 Finances/accounts/orders based in India.
9 Initial sales aimed at EU countries and the USA.
10 Distributed in Britain from headquarters in Birmingham.
11 Trainers sold in a chain of shops throughout the UK.

about the high-pressure environment and the **sweatshop** conditions, were denied trade union rights and sacked.

Shane doesn't want to be the odd one out and he remembers that last term one of his friends was being constantly laughed at because of the cheap trainers he wore.

? Questions

1 How would you describe a good citizen? Why do we need good citizens?
2 Why are the choices and decisions we make so important?
3 Describe some of the ways in which you might be influenced when making decisions.
4 Explain what you would do if you were in Shane's position. Give reasons for your opinion.

GLOSSARY

Eco-friendly: A term given to products that do little or no damage to the environment.

Peers: A group of young people of similar age.

Sweatshops: A factory where workers endure long hours, low wages and poor conditions.

Rights and Responsibilities

KEY ISSUES

○ What are the legal and moral rights and responsibilities of:
a) Parents
b) Teachers
c) Students?

▲ Special officers look for children who should be at school.

Sandy says that she would rather be anywhere than at school. She has few friends, complains that she gets picked on and finds learning difficult. Whenever possible she tries to miss lessons. She uses many excuses, including telling her mum that she has a throat infection, a headache, a temperature or earache, and sometimes she visits the park or the shops rather than attend school. On other occasions she throws a tantrum and refuses to go. The school is very concerned that Sandy is getting further behind with her school work and the Education Welfare Officer has called several times but still the situation has not improved. This morning Sandy's mum received a letter threatening court action and Sandy was found hiding in the local park by a police constable and taken to school.

Darrell is in his final year at primary school. In September, the Local Education Authority (LEA) expects him to attend the secondary school that is within 1.5 km of his home but there are two comprehensives in the town. With his parents he attended the open evenings at both of them and he was particularly impressed with the facilities offered by the school across town. Darrell loves music and computers and the Community College that is about 6.5 km away has an impressive orchestra and numerous computers of the very latest specifications

i INFO BOX

The 1996 Education Act states that it is the duty of parents to ensure that their child has *'an efficient full-time education suitable to his or her age, ability and aptitude … by regular attendance at school or otherwise'*.

Compulsory school age is from the first term after the student's fifth birthday until the last Friday in June of the school year in which they are 16. Parents can be prosecuted and fined if their son or daughter does not attend school or receive an education elsewhere. In such a situation it is not a defence to say that they did not know that their child was playing truant or that they could not get them to attend.

The 1998 Crime and Disorder Act gave the police authority to take children back to school if they found them playing truant.

Schools have a legal duty to try to prevent bullying and must publish a policy on their procedures to deal with it.

What are the legal and moral rights and responsibilities of parents, student and the school in situations like this?

with internet access. The school nearest him has an equally good reputation concerning examination results and nearly all his friends will be going there.

 What factors should Darrell and his parents consider when deciding which school to apply for?

 INFO BOX

The 1980 Education Act gives the right of choice to parents regarding the school they wish their child to attend. If they choose a school that is full or if it is a church school the admission may be refused.

Parents, by law, should be asked to sign a **home-school agreement** but they have the right to refuse to sign it if they are not in favour of the conditions that it contains.

A Typical Home–School Agreement

The staff and governors at the school will endeavour to:

- Provide a balanced curriculum and meet the individual needs of the student.
- Ensure that the student reaches her or his full potential as a valued member of the school community.
- Encourage the student to achieve high standards of work and behaviour by building good relationships.
- Keep parents informed about general school matters and, in particular, about their own son or daughter's progress.
- Be open and welcoming at all times and offer opportunities for parents to become involved in daily life at the school.

Parents will endeavour to:

- Ensure their son or daughter attends school regularly, on time and equipped for each day's learning.
- Make the school aware of concerns or problems which may affect the student's learning.
- Support the school's policy on behaviour.
- Support the student in homework and other opportunities for home learning.
- Attend parents' evenings and discussions about student's progress.

Students will endeavour to:

- Arrive at school on time and equipped for the day's lessons.
- Adhere to the school rules and the School Code of Conduct.

- Wear the school uniform and be tidy in appearance at all times.
- Be polite and helpful.

 PROJECT WORK

Discuss the main responsibilities for parents, teachers and students included in the home-school agreement.

Teachers take on the responsibility of acting as parents while students are in their care. This is known as *in loco parentis*.

▲ Teachers *in loco parentis* on a field trip.

GLOSSARY

Loco parentis: Acting as parents in the absence of your parents. The term is used to describe the legal responsibility of teachers.

Home–school agreement: A formal agreement in writing between parents and a school stating the rights and responsibilities of each partner to the agreement.

 Questions

1 Explain the issues that Sandy's situation brings to light.
2 What do you think should be done in Sandy's case?
3 Explain why the right to the choice of school could be important in both Sandy and Darrell's situations.
4 What arguments would you use to suggest that a home-school agreement might help to encourage a partnership between parents, teachers and students?
5 Explain what is meant by *in loco parentis*.

Rights and Responsibilities

Is it Fair?

The rules in Victorian schools were very strict and reflected the belief that '*children should be seen but not heard*'. Some examples of the rules include:

Children must:

- Stand up when an adult enters the room.
- Call teachers 'Sir' or 'Ma'am'.
- Not ask questions.
- Stand up straight to answer a teacher's question.
- Be silent unless given permission to speak.
- Sit up straight in lessons
- Write using the right hand only.
- Not count using their fingers

Children will be caned if they

- Do poor work.
- Talk in class.
- Fidget.
- Miss school (truant).
- Are late for school.

Were These Rules Fair on the Students?

Rules about the school uniform often bring heated debate and discussion.

The uniform of a school is usually agreed after discussions with governors, staff and parents. Every school has the right to insist that students wear a uniform providing it is reasonable. Failure to wear the agreed uniform may result in the offender being sent home. The parents could face a fine for their child's non-attendance if this situation happened frequently. Teachers may confiscate jewellery that is not allowed as part of the school uniform (usually because of health and safety reasons) but students have a right to have it back after the school day has ended.

Uniform Protest

One sweltering summer term Friday, some students refused to return to lessons after morning break because they wanted the right to wear short trousers. The fire alarm was set off and many pupils sat down on the playing fields and refused to move. A few picked up rounders bats which were being used by a P.E. class and the police were called to help calm down the situation.

The school uniform consists of blue sweatshirts or light blue polo shirts and long black trousers, but not shorts. Governors might have been persuaded that shorts were a reasonable option in hot weather, but the students did not go through the school council or the correct channels.

The head teacher permanently excluded two boys and a girl, with another four being excluded for up to two weeks and many more for five days or less.

Julie, a 15-year-old student, was sent home because she had a tongue stud fitted on holiday. She was told not to come back to school until she had removed the stud.

▲ A typical Victorian classroom.

▲ Students have been suspended because of the style of their hair cut or their hair colouring.

Why do schools have rules about uniform if it often results in controversy?

LOCKED OUT

It was wet, cold and windy. Lisa was famished and the dining hall was full, so she went to her form room. There she opened a packet of crisps and, unnoticed by a dozen of her classmates, she quietly began to enjoy them. She knew that no eating or drinking was allowed in the form room, but she was being very careful. Then suddenly a teacher's voice echoed across the room. Lisa jumped as she heard her name being spoken and crisps scattered on the floor. *'You've broken the rules Lisa, the whole class is locked out. Everyone out now, I'm locking the door!' 'But, why us sir,'* chorused the rest of the group, *'we weren't breaking any rules.' 'Haven't you heard of collective responsibility?'* came the reply.

Education costs taxpayers billions of pounds each year and so annual tuition fees have been introduced for university students. The government says that once the students have graduated, they are likely to earn high wages and should be able to pay off the debts they incur as a result of attending university. Students do not usually see it this way.

Student Action

On 1 March 2001, many university students protested to highlight their financial problems. Some formed a human-chain in south London along the bus route linking Goldsmiths College with Lewisham College of Further Education. Their aim was to show that the journey from further to higher education is the most expensive one students will ever make. In other parts of the country students wore black armbands or wrote their debts on cards and attached them to balloons to send up in the sky. In Birmingham, students staged a cardboard city sleep out to raise awareness of the cost of their accommodation. Others wrote to MPs, the media and other groups in the community, asking for support.

 INFO BOX

In England, Wales and Northern Ireland university students pay a means-tested annual fee of £1050 (2000–1 figure). There are now no upfront fees in Scotland, instead graduates make contributions from their earnings. Students are able to borrow nearly £3500 a year under a loan repayment scheme. Once in employment and when their earnings reach what is called the threshold level (currently £14,000 a year) they start repayments. The amount to be repaid includes interest charged at the rate of inflation. It is estimated that students on average have debts of over £12,000 when they graduate.

GLOSSARY

Collective responsibility: The group as a whole is answerable and accountable for their actions. There is a shared duty.

▲ Students protesting about their financial problems.

? Questions

1 How are the Victorian school rules different from school rules today?
2 Why do you think that school rules have changed since the Victorian times?
3 Do you think it fair that students are made to wear school uniform?
4 Was it fair that all the class were locked out of a classroom because of one individual's action?
5 What did the teacher mean when he mentioned 'collective responsibility'?
6 How might students influence government decisions?

School Rules

School Rules

KEY ISSUES

○ How is power and authority exercised within school?
○ How can students influence decisions that are taken in schools?

Who Runs the School?

Secondary schools have numerous employees (teachers, administration staff, learning assistants, technicians, caretakers, cleaners), six-figure budgets and responsibility for the school buildings. They provide a service for hundreds of students and many other learning opportunities for their local communities. The Ofsted inspectors measure the quality of their provision. The key contributing groups in the running of the schools are the managers (including the head teacher and senior management team), governors, staff, students and parents.

The Role of Governors

Parent governors are elected by parents of the students at the school. The governing body of the school is made up of:

- Parent governors elected by the parents of the students at the school.
- Local Education Authority appointments.
- Teacher governors elected by the teaching staff.
- The head teacher.
- A staff governor elected by the non-teaching staff (optional for small governing bodies).
- The governors may co-opt additional members.

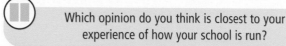

Which opinion do you think is closest to your experience of how your school is run?

Governors have responsibility for determining, monitoring and keeping under review the broad policies, plans and procedures within which the school operates. They share the responsibility for employment of the staff and it is their job to seek to maintain and develop the ethos and reputation of the school.

The Head Teacher/Principal and Staff

There are different styles of management within schools, but the head teacher is responsible for the implementation of policy, day-to-day management of the school and the operation of the curriculum. He or she is responsible for the leadership and direction of the school and is accountable to the governing body and the Local Education Authority. To help with this, the head usually has a management team that includes deputy heads with particular areas of responsibility, for instance, pastoral deputy, curriculum deputy. This group usually makes the main **executive decisions** concerning the running of the school.

Middle managers assist with the subject or pastoral areas and all staff have the opportunity of expressing their views and concerns at staff meetings. Other committees or working parties exist in most schools giving teachers the opportunity to influence policies and decisions. Often a **consensus** may be sought rather than the imposition of a management decision.

Pupil Power
School Councils
Most schools recognise that each student has a stake in what happens to them while they are being educated and they try to involve pupils in decision making. This may be done through questionnaires, discussion groups or school or class councils.

Approximately 50 per cent of secondary schools have a school council. Elected class representatives meet on a regular basis with members of the senior management team and discuss issues that affect the school. Students are given the opportunity to become actively engaged in democracy, and regardless of their age, ability, or personality, they may make a positive contribution to their school community.

▲ A school council meeting.

As **stakeholders**, schools councils give students:
- A voice in the running of the school.
- An opportunity to experience democracy in action.
- An opportunity to develop a partnership between staff and pupils.
- An opportunity to develop positive peer leadership.
- An opportunity to make a positive contribution to the school.
- An opportunity to develop debating skills and the ability to put across a point of view.

Items for discussion often include the school's catering, extra curricular opportunities, raising work for charity, anti-bullying policies and various school facilities.

Sometimes students feel frustrated that they are unable to change things overnight, but an insight is given into how running a school community works.

Class Councils
Some schools have taken democracy a stage further by organising class councils. This provides a structure for each student to take part in decision making within the school. In their tutor groups, the students are able to discuss classroom issues and to raise concerns that they want their class representatives to bring up at the school council. New school policies may be discussed, for example, proposals to change the school uniform or code of conduct.

Parents
Parents are also concerned about the education provided by the local school. Parents are able to express their views at meetings, such as parents' meetings, and can bring pressure for change if they feel that it is necessary.

GLOSSARY

Consensus: Agreement between everyone, rather than needing to take a vote or someone to make a decision one way or the other.

Executive decisions: The controlling group (management) make a ruling or policy.

Stakeholder: As a member of the school community, each student has an interest in what happens and what decisions are made because it affects them.

? Questions

1 What role do the governors have in the running of a school?
2 Explain the powers and responsibilities of a head teacher?
3 To what extent might students take part in school policy making?
4 How might school councils help promote cooperation within a school?
5 What arguments would you put forward to encourage students to become involved in class councils?

School Rules

KEY ISSUES

- How are schools involved with the local community?
- What can the local communities and schools offer each other?
- What opportunities are there for involvement in local issues?

Getting Involved with the Community

Community Colleges

Many secondary schools are also **community** colleges. Education is not limited to 9 a.m to 4 p.m. for students aged 11–18, but classes for adults may also exist during the day and they continue during the evenings. Adult classes give learning opportunities to those of all ages in the community. Adults are given the chance to improve their skills at a wide range of subjects from learning foreign languages or how to use computers, to gardening and basket making. When the day teaching staff go home, a whole new group of tutors arrive to take charge of the evening activities. Most of these activities are self-financing because those who attend pay course fees, but often the school benefits through extra facilities being provided. For example, some community colleges have dual-purpose libraries. This means that the public use it as well as students, but it has more books and other resources than a normal school library.

▲ Students and adults at an evening class.

Community Schemes

Schools are part of the local, national and international communities and can benefit from being involved in local issues and projects. Many schools offer students the opportunity to become involved in community schemes, such as environmental projects. For example, in the Spring of 2001, Waverley Borough involved their local schools in a scheme to plant a native British tree in their grounds to mark the millennium. Thirty-nine schools took up the offer, which was supported by the Mayor and the World Wildlife Fund. The project helped to raise awareness of issues associated with the environment, including global warming.

 How could students become involved in community issues or projects?

Working Together

Students at a rural school expressed their desire to use a swimming pool. The nearest pool was many kilometres away and several students had never had the opportunity to learn to swim. One of the class representatives raised the matter at a school council meeting and found a great deal of interest and initial support from both the staff and student representatives. Members of the local community were approached, including councillors, parents, various youth organisations, the local primary schools and businesses. Grants were obtained and sponsorship received from local businesses. As a result a project began, which built a pool at the school and parents and the community were actively involved in the construction. Now students at the secondary school and children from the primary schools use the pool. Outside of school hours members of the community are able to make use of the facility.

 How did the students benefit from having a school council and then working with the community?

From Local to International

The charity 'Send a Cow' originally began to send pregnant heifers to Uganda to help improve the country's livestock. Since then, 'Send a Cow' has expanded to help those involved in agriculture in many ways. Schemes include the provision of goats,

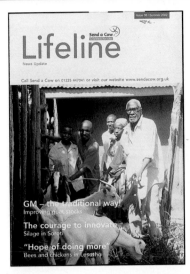

▲ The 'Send a Cow' newsletter keeps supporters informed.

pigs and bees (for honey production). David Bragg, the current chair of the 'Send a Cow' trustees, made his local secondary school aware of the links that were being forged.

Fund-raising events for the charity were organised and connections were made with the local churches. As a result, in 1999, Denis Kigongo, a former teacher from Kampala in Uganda, came to Devon. Most weekdays Denis worked at the Community College in Chulmleigh, assisting teachers in the classroom and organising activities such as a Christian Union and assemblies, and he set up an African drum group (*Sanyu*).

The project expanded further when the idea of taking the African drum group and other students to Uganda and the development of an exchange with African young people and teachers was conceived. Members of the community were invited to join, which had the benefit of ensuring that the adult–student ratio was as small as possible (1:3). One of the parents, a local doctor, and two nurses were attracted by the opportunity to visit Ugandan medical facilities. A range of activities resulted as students, parents and members of the community got involved before the visit to Uganda in February 2002. Fund-raising events, including school discos, were organised by staff and parents. Students took part in music concerts and a Ugandan theme day for the pupils took place. Links were made with Ugandan primary and secondary schools and clothing and toys were collected for an orphanage. A visit was made to a village that had been helped by 'Send a Cow' and sports equipment was taken to help the Ugandan Youth Outreach project. A reception was held at the British High Commission and the group visited museums, the source of the Nile and went on safari.

GLOSSARY

Community: A geographical area and the people who live there. An individual feels a sense of belonging to and shares a common identity.

? Questions

1. What benefits might a secondary school gain from being a community college?
2. How might students be involved in community schemes or projects?
3. How might involvement with the local community help a school?
4. Explain some of the benefits that the Community College at Chulmleigh might obtain from its link with 'Send a Cow', the local churches and Uganda.
5. What links does your school have with the local community?

▲ Sanyu

Equality and Diversity

KEY ISSUES

- What does the law say about equal opportunities?
- How can schools promote equal opportunities for all?

Equal Opportunities

The Human Rights Act of 1998 stated that everyone should have the right not to be treated differently because of their race, religion, sex, political views or any other status, unless this can be justified objectively. This means that everyone should be treated the same and given **equal opportunities** regardless of their background or beliefs unless there is an extremely good reason in a specific circumstance for not doing so.

The Sex Discrimination Act of 1975 produced major changes in the practices in schools. The Act requires schools to treat girls and boys equally. In particular this means providing equal access to the main curriculum and to curricular options. No longer could schools insist that boys should have different options from girls. A hundred years ago a typical school might have the following rules:
Boys will:
- Learn technical drawing.
- Line up separately from girls.
Girls will:
- Learn needlework and cooking
- Wear their hair tied back.

At that time men were expected to be the wage earners, while women remained at home and brought up the family. Schools are now expected to give students the opportunity to challenge traditional views of career options and **stereotyping**. Research shows that many girls still leave school with low career aspirations. Girls and boys usually make stereotypical choices of options and subjects.

Traditionally, for example, few girls have been attracted to working in the world of physics, engineering and technology. Schools can raise the profile of these subjects for girls through careers guidance, opportunities for work experience, links with industry and role models. Mentors (sometimes described as advisers or counsellors) are used in some schools to attract more girls into less traditional areas. Some schools have invited recently graduated women science students to speak to the

▲ A female engineer showing NASA spacecraft models.

students. Some universities, including the University of Sunderland, have developed a scheme where undergraduates are sponsored to work in schools to help with science projects.

 Is it right to make assumptions that girls will be interested in different subjects and careers than boys?

Expectations

Stephen Byers, a former government minister, said '*We ... should not simply accept with a shrug of our shoulders that boys will be boys.*' He was referring to the gender difference in examination results. In some areas of the country up to 15 per cent more girls achieve five or more GCSEs at Grade C or above compared to boys. Statistics show that boys are underachieving as a group compared with girls at all levels.

Many say that this is because of the 'laddish, anti-learning' culture among boys who regard it as 'sissy' to appear to want to learn. Over 80 per cent of students excluded from school are boys and research has shown that many more detentions are given to boys than girls. Others may argue that teachers tend to pick on the boys and allow girls off more easily.

A number of schools are looking to develop strategies to improve boys' achievement without putting girls at a disadvantage. Research has shown that most boys learn better by doing practical and active tasks rather than just listening to what the teacher tells them. Studies suggest that boys respond better to short-term tasks where the lessons are broken up into steps.

> Is it fair to label boys as underachievers? Do you think that there is any truth in the idea that teachers seem to favour girls and rarely blame them for disruptive behaviour?

Disability Discrimination

The provisions of the Special Educational Needs and Disability Discrimination Act 2001 came into force on 1 September 2002. This made it unlawful to discriminate against adults or students with disabilities by treating them less favourably than anyone else. Governors must publish information in their annual report concerning arrangements for disabled students.

Special Needs

A student is defined as having special educational needs (SEN) if he or she has a learning difficulty that requires special educational provision to be made for him or her. All state schools must have a special needs coordinator (SENCO) who is responsible for the day-to-day operation of the school's SEN policy. Often classroom assistants help to provide additional support so that the SEN students can engage in all of the school's regular activities.

Religious Understanding

The religious traditions in Britain are, in the main, Christian. However, there are sizeable minorities from the other major world religions. Some faith groups (including Christian, Muslim and Jewish communities) would like more schools for students who belong exclusively to their particular religion. Under the Education Act 1996, Religious Education must be provided in Local Education Authority and voluntary controlled schools. This is provided through the Locally Agreed Syllabus. Unlike other subjects on the curriculum, each LEA discusses what Religious Education should be provided in their area. Representatives from the different faith communities participate in the working parties that draw up these syllabuses. This gives R.E. an important role in promoting understanding between different religious groups by showing the richness of a diversity of cultures and beliefs. Parents do have the right to request the withdrawal of their child from part or all religious education.

GLOSSARY

Equal opportunities: The opportunity or right to be offered choice without discrimination on grounds of gender, race, religion, disability, etc.

Stereotyping: A building of an image of a group of people, which is based on prejudice or on an over-simplified idea.

▲ A Muslim school in London.

? Questions

1. What does the Human Rights Act of 1998 state about equal opportunities?
2. What difference has the Sex Discrimination Act of 1975 made to the opportunities of boys and girls at school?
3. What do schools have to do for those students with special needs or disabilities?
4. Why are state schools required to teach students about different religions?
5. Do you think that it is a good idea for different religious groups to have their own faith schools?

Equality and Diversity

KEY ISSUES

❍ What is meant by a multicultural society?
❍ How do cultural differences provide challenges and opportunities?
❍ How do we overcome racial prejudice?

▲ Martin Luther King – American Civil Rights Leader.

Our Multicultural Society

Britain has become a multicultural society. This means that within Britain there are many different cultural groups. Over many centuries people from most parts of the world have migrated to this country bringing with them their literature, arts, music, religion, language, customs, traditions and skills. This has meant that Britain has a great deal of diversity and a richness of culture. It gives schools the opportunity to provide education to help young people to understand the values, customs and beliefs of many of the different people of the world.

There are many reasons why people have come to Britain. People have:

• Come to seek asylum (safety from persecution).
• Been invited because of their skills.
• Dual citizenship and/or are from the Commonwealth.
• Looked for an opportunity to experience a better quality of life

Having a multicultural society brings its challenges as well as opportunities (see pages 26–27). One of the major challenges is to overcome resentment and **prejudice** and to promote respect and understanding. In England as a whole, minority ethnic groups make up 11.3 per cent of the population of schools that are funded through the Local Education Authorities. However, there are enormous variations. One school in east London had a sixth form of 125 pupils of whom only one was white; while less than one in 500 pupils is black in Cornwall and the Isles of Scilly.

Martin Luther King summed up the challenge when he was talking about American society, '*I have a dream that my four little children will one day live in a nation where they will not be judged according to the colour of their skin but by the content of their character.*'

 INFO BOX

RACE RELATIONS

The Race Relations Act of 1976 made it illegal for schools to **discriminate** against anyone on the grounds of colour, race, nationality, ethnic or national origins. The Act applies not only to education but also to jobs, housing, training, and the provision of goods, facilities and services. Schools must not decide to refuse admission on grounds of race or sex (although the Sex Discrimination Act of 1985 does permit single-sex schools). Schools are required to have a written policy on race equality and assess the impact of their policies on minority ethnic students and staff.

The Race Relations (Amendment) Act 2000 made it clear that racist incidents ranging from harassment and abuse to physical violence are offences under the criminal law. Provoking racial hatred is also an offence, including published material such as leaflets or newspapers.

▲ 'He helped himself to my chocolate biscuits!'

INFO BOX

RACIAL PREJUDICE
Racial prejudice involves holding opinions or attitudes about people because of their racial or ethnic origin, based on false assumptions or inadequate evidence. It involves prejudging people, intolerance and unfairness. Racial prejudice usually involves ignorance, despising someone who is different than ourselves and thinking badly about someone for no real reason.

Tina's Mistake

Tina's last lesson had been P.E. It was break time but she was late from having a shower and getting changed. She rushed to the cafeteria exhausted and desperate for some refreshments. The cafeteria was teeming with other students but she managed to purchase a drink and a packet of chocolate biscuits. She slumped into the last seat, relieved to be able to sit at last but uneasy that she was sitting next to a male Indian student. She opened the biscuits, took one and began her drink. The Indian student on her table gave her a big smile and helped himself to one of the biscuits. She was fuming that he had taken one of her biscuits but she was aware of some of the racial tensions in the school and so she said nothing. She just ate her biscuit and took another. Imagine her surprise when the Indian took one. She bit her tongue and looked the other way. Then to her amazement he took the last chocolate biscuit out of the packet, broke it in half and with a big smile on his face he offered her one part of it. Although furious she just took it, finished her drink and headed off quickly to her next lesson. Once in the lesson, she complained bitterly to her best friends about what had happened. Some of her comments were racist but she suddenly stopped in mid-sentence because as she opened her bag to get out her exercise book, there right on top, were her chocolate biscuits. Whose biscuits had she eaten?

 How do you think Tina felt when she discovered her mistake?

GLOSSARY

Discrimination: Action taken against a group. In the negative sense this is because of prejudice, e.g. refusal to give a person a job because they come from a particular racial group. Positive discrimination may be used to ensure fair treatment for groups who might otherwise lose out.

Pluralist society: A form of society with many minority cultures or groups.

Prejudice: Prejudging before a proper examination of the facts has taken place.

Xenophobia: A fear, hatred or distrust of foreigners.

Questions

1 Why does Britain have so many different cultures?
2 Explain the challenges and opportunities of living in a multicultural society.
3 Has Martin Luther King's dream become a reality in Britain? Give reasons for your opinion.
4 What does the 1976 Race Relations Act say about discrimination?
5 What does Tina's story show us about prejudice and jumping to conclusions?

Rights and Responsibilities

KEY ISSUES

○ What rights and responsibilities do employers and employees have?
○ What laws exist to help ensure that everyone has equal opportunities at work?

Sadie has been working part-time at Mr Duckworth's grocery shop for two years. She is one of 12 workers but is the only one who is black. Sadie was very happy until Mr Duckworth decided to open on Sundays and he tells Sadie that she must work every Sunday morning. Sadie refuses because she is deeply religious and wishes to attend church with her family. Mr Duckworth tells her that she is sacked. Sadie feels unfairly treated but what can she do?

From the first day of employment the law guarantees certain rights. These include the right to:
• Join a **trade union**.
• Time off for public duties.
• Equal pay.
• Eighteen weeks' maternity leave.
• Non-discrimination on the basis of race, disability and sex.

Having worked one month, **employees** are entitled to:
• Payment if they are laid off.
• A week's notice of dismissal.

Having worked two months, employees are entitled to:
• A written statement of the main terms of employment.

After one year's employment, employees are entitled to:
• Protection against being dismissed unfairly.

Employees are also entitled to **redundancy pay** based on the employee's age, how long the employee has worked continuously for the employer (after reaching the age of 18) and the employee's weekly pay. If 20 or more employees are being made **redundant** within 90 days, then the company must consult representatives from the employees about the proposed redundancy measures.

Part-time workers have the same rights as full-time employees. They should receive all benefits, including holidays, on a pro-rata basis.

 INFO BOX

The Sunday Trading Act of 1994 gave shop workers the right not to be dismissed or selected for redundancy for refusing to work on Sundays.

The Race Relations Act of 1976 made it illegal for employers to discriminate against anyone on the grounds of colour, race, nationality, ethnic or national origins.

Trade Unions

An employee may join a trade union and, if he or she believes that they are being unfairly treated, they can seek help from the trade union representative. The union representative will try to resolve the situation with the manager or employer. Failure to sort out the problem may lead to the matter being taken to an industrial tribunal. It is unlawful for employers to penalise or dismiss (or threaten to dismiss) staff because of their trade union membership or to try to prevent them from joining a union.

Narinder has worked in the same company for over 20 years. She is extremely well qualified and has an unblemished record. To begin with she obtained the promotions that her experience and qualifications merited. As she got nearer the top of the company there appeared to be a reluctance to consider her for future promotions. Men with less experience and

INFO BOX

The Disability Discrimination Act of 1995 aimed to introduce measures to stop discrimination against people with disabilities. The employment provisions of the Act does not apply to firms with fewer than 15 employees, the Armed Forces, prison officers, firefighters, the police force, and those who work on board ships and aircraft. Under the Act employers may have to make adjustments to premises, modify equipment, provide supervision and allocate some of the employee's duties to another person.

fewer qualifications were given the jobs for which she applied. Narinder became suspicious that she was being discriminated against because of her gender.

 Is it possible that Narinder could do anything about it?

 INFO BOX

The Sex Discrimination Act of 1975 made it unlawful to treat a person less favourably because of their sex. The Equal Pay Act of 1970 was introduced to make it unlawful to offer different pay and conditions to men and women who are doing the same or similar work, or are rated at the same level in their employment.

National Minimum Wage

The government introduced a national minimum wage because they wished to protect people from being underpaid. Approximately one in 12 workers benefit from it, which is around 1.9 million in total. The rate in 2002 was over £4 per hour for those over 21 and covers the following:

- Full-time, part-time and casual workers.
- Home and freelance workers.
- Temporary and agency workers.
- Pensioners (if they are working).
- Piece workers.

Craig, who is 22, has a job in a local factory. He works extremely long hours because his pay is very poor and the factory owner says that he is unable to pay more than £3.90 an hour because profits are so low. He says that if he is forced to pay more then he will have to sack some of his employees. Craig does not believe that this is true and feels that he is being

treated unfairly because he works at least ten hours overtime every week and does not get paid for it. He does not want to lose his job, but he is not prepared to allow things to continue as they are.

 What advice would you give Craig?

GLOSSARY

Employee: A person who works for someone in return for wages.

Employer: A person or company who employs people.

Redundancy: The dismissal of an employee because there is a need to cut jobs, move the place of work or close down completely.

Redundancy payment: Employees may be entitled to a lump-sum payment from employers when they are made redundant.

Trade Union: An organisation, which has been formed to improve workers' pay and conditions.

? **Questions**

1. Consider Sadie's situation. If Mr Duckworth sacks her would he be breaking any law? Give reasons for your answer.
2. Apart from protection from unfair dismissal, what other rights does the law give to employees?
3. What is meant by redundancy and redundancy payments?
4. Explain what the law says about equal pay and equal opportunities for men and women.
5. Why is Craig's employer breaking the law?

KEY ISSUES

○ What are the employers' responsibilities concerning health and safety?
○ What actions can be taken to protect workers?

Two workers died from heat exposure at Harvestine Bakery in Leicester in 1998. The management had received a quote from the manufacturers of around £2500 to carry out repairs to their giant oven. Thinking this excessive, they decided to use their own workforce to do the repairs. Only about two hours was allowed for the giant oven to cool down. Two men went to their deaths as they entered the still blistering hot bread oven. It was reported that Leicester Crown Court imposed fines totalling £628,000 on the company, two of its directors and a manager.

The 1974 Health and Safety at Work Act made it the responsibility of employers to look after the safety of their employees. Section 2 (2) (e) made it compulsory for employers to ensure:

'*The provision and maintenance of a working environment for his employees that is, so far as is reasonably practicable, safe without risks to health, and adequate as regards facilities and arrangement for their welfare at work.*'

Employees have the right to expect employers to have taken every reasonable precaution to look after their health and safety. For example, it is the duty of a company to erect guards on dangerous moving machinery. Employees need protection from accidentally getting caught up in the machinery.

A 29-year-old paper maker was killed at Burnley Paper and Board Mill in Lancashire. He was attempting to clean a paper machine when it was working at full speed and no safety guards had been provided. As a result, the company Smurfit UK Ltd was fined £100,000.

The Reporting of Injuries, Diseases and Dangerous Occurrences Regulations 1995 made it compulsory for employers to notify the Health and Safety Executive or local authority about work accidents where an employee is off work more than three days.

Of the 295 who died in 2000–1 (see the bar chart), 106 were in the construction industry and 46 in agriculture. Seventy-three fatalities were the result of falls from heights, 64 from moving vehicles, 52 from falling and moving objects and 37 by objects collapsing or overturning.

The Management of Health and Safety at Work Regulations 1992 made it a requirement that employers have to provide risk assessments, which include noise levels (The Noise at Work Regulations 1989). Once the decibels exceed about 83 there is a risk to health, and over 100 the sound levels become

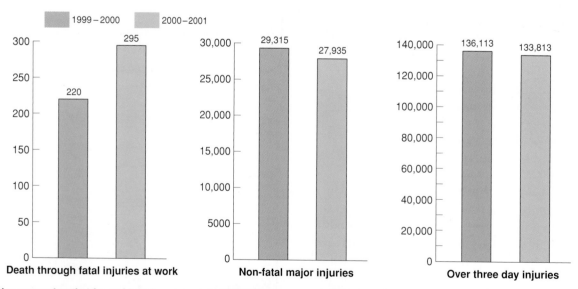

▲ Statistics comparing deaths and injuries at work in 1999/2000 compared with 2000/2001.

◄ Health and safety issues are very important in many occupations.

obtain an apprenticeship in engineering when she leaves school. During the day she becomes aware that there are many hazards in her new working environment. These include obstructions in corridors, pieces of metal (which could cause her to trip) and machinery that she has never used, welding equipment and the like. She has been asked to move some heavy metal and to attempt some welding. Her immediate reaction is to be worried because she is not sure she can cope with the lifting, she has done very little welding before, and she does not know where the protective clothing is kept or where there is a fire extinguisher.

harmful. For example, noise levels from a jet engine reach 140 and it is essential for workers to wear clothing to protect their ears.

Hazardous substances also need to be handled carefully and employers have a duty to identify any such substances in their companies by completing a control of substances hazardous to health regulations (**COSHH**) survey. For some very dangerous substances there are specific regulations, for instance, the Control of Asbestos at Work Regulations 1992. Many workers who were exposed to asbestos before the current legislation have suffered severe health problems from asbestosis, mesothelioma and lung cancer. Where a company has been found to be at fault, sufferers may have been awarded **compensation** for their illness. Around 1800 deaths from mesothelioma and asbestosis were recorded in 1999.

Employees also have a duty to '*take reasonable care of the health and safety of themselves and others who may be affected by their acts or omissions at work*' (Section 7 of the 1974 Health and Safety at Work Act).

❚❚ In practice what does this duty of looking after yourself and others mean?

Work Experience Safety Issues

Julie is determined to create a good impression on her first day at a local garage. She has been looking forward to her work experience placement for some time. This is particularly because she wishes to

GLOSSARY

Compensation: Money given as payment for loss of employment or damage or injury.

COSHH: Acronym for Control of Substances Hazardous to Health.

❓ Questions

1 Which Act made it the responsibility of employers to look after the safety of their employees? What does the Act require employers to do?
2 According to the chart on page 20 what are the main causes of fatalities at work?
3 Explain, with examples, some of the long-term hazards to health that are faced by some workers.
4 Faced with the situation of her work experience what do you think Julie should do? Give reasons for your opinion.

Work in Motion

KEY ISSUES

○ How does a business contribute to the local and national economy?
○ How do individuals and businesses use financial services?

Work and the Economy

1 The development of the chip

Anne-Marie's work experience placement was in a local factory that makes microchips for computers. During her stay she was given a lesson in the history of the chip and an insight into the impact this invention has made on the modern world. In 1959, Jack Kilby, an American engineer, developed a small, self-contained, 'monolithic' integrated circuit in a single piece of semiconductor material about the size of a fingernail. The microchip made microprocessors possible and, therefore, allowed high-speed computing and communications systems to become efficient, convenient and affordable.

2 The company's organisation

Anne-Marie's placement was mainly in the administration side of the firm and she was able to see how the company supplies several other businesses with the microchip. In their industrial units, the chip is assembled with many other parts to create computers. She was amazed to find that the product, having been made locally, was taken to many factories throughout Britain and exported to countries throughout the world. The firm employs hundreds of people with the necessary skills, which include making the chip, dealing with the customers, arranging the transport and finance. On one occasion Anne-Marie was given an opportunity to see how the stock control was organised and on her final day she worked in the wages department. There she saw the wage slips being prepared for those on the payroll and she realised that the company pays hundreds of thousands of pounds in total every week to the workers.

3 The local community

It was clear to Anne-Marie that this company plays a vital part in the local community. Not only does it provide employment but also it generates wealth in the area. Much of the employees' wages gets spent in the locality, e.g. in the shops, on entertainment and on accommodation. Workers spend their wages supporting their families and local businesses benefit from the millions that are paid out. If the company moved, closed or made workers redundant the knock-on effect on many businesses would be enormous. Many would find it difficult to survive because they have become dependent on the custom of the factory workers. On the other hand, if the company expands further, then local businesses would gain extra trade and income and new businesses might start up as a result.

4 Taxes

While in the finance department, Anne-Marie noticed that the employees had deductions taken out of their wages and she asked her supervisor why this happened. She was informed that the deductions include income tax and National Insurance contributions. The money raised from this goes to the government and is used to provide services such as the National Health Service, the armed forces and the state retirement pension. Other taxes are not taken directly from the wage packet, such as Value Added Tax (VAT) and the Council Tax. VAT is paid when purchasing goods and services. Council Tax is a local taxation system, introduced 1 April 1993 to replace the previous and unpopular community charge (poll tax). This tax, based on the property value, is used to provide local services such as education, police and the maintenance of roads. Each worker contributes through his or her taxes to the provision of local and national services.

5 Financial services

Anne-Marie discovered that the company she worked for had a turnover of millions of pounds each year. **Shareholders** have invested in the company and they benefit from profits because they are paid an annual **dividend**, and sometimes workers receive a bonus if their productivity is high and targets have been met. The company relies heavily on banking facilities and electronic funds transfers when doing financial deals. This includes calculating deals in foreign currencies, such as the Euro, and transferring money in and out of their accounts. Accountants are employed by the company to help ensure that the accounts are kept in order. Each year an **audit** of the accounts has to be prepared and checked before it can be presented to shareholders. Sometimes loans are required to finance large deals or the expansion of the company. Banks are usually willing to lend money but the company has to pay back this capital (as it is called) over a set period of time, plus any interest that the banks charge it. Many of the workers have a mortgage on their homes. They have borrowed money from the bank or a mortgage society in order to gradually pay for the property (most people do it over 25 years). Other loans may have been obtained, e.g. to purchase a car. Most make use of credit cards or bankers' cheques to pay for their bills to avoid carrying large quantities of cash with them. Electronic fund transfer systems can move funds locally, nationally or internationally in a matter of seconds. When on holiday in another country, a charge card such as Visa can withdraw money in the local currency.

Anne-Marie's work experience placement shows the way that work affects the economy and this is applicable to all companies.

GLOSSARY

Audit: An official examination of accounts to see that they are correct.

Dividends: A share of the company's profits which is paid to shareholders.

Shareholders: A person who owns shares in a business or company.

 ## Questions

1 Explain the effect of the business where Anne-Marie worked, on:
   a) The individual worker.
   b) The local community.
2 How does this company and other firms contribute towards the provision of national services?
3 Why is it important for towns to have a variety of industries?
4 How does the company where Anne-Marie worked and its workforce make use of financial services?

 ## PROJECT WORK

Why might it be financially dangerous for a town to become too reliant on just one main industry to support it?

The Business World

KEY ISSUES

○ How do firms relate to other businesses?
○ How do businesses provide employment and benefit the country's economy?

A strong economy is important for the country because it provides opportunities to employ more people. When an economy declines, output of goods, services and incomes also decline, and there are fewer opportunities for employment. Sometimes one part of the economy declines but another part expands. For example, in Britain traditional industries like steel, shipbuilding and fishing have

▲ Open cast mining – an example of a primary industry.

▲ A textile factory – an example of a secondary industry.

▲ Tourism – an example of a service or tertiary industry.

declined in recent years but the service industry and new technologies have grown. Work is usually classified into primary industry (mining and agriculture), secondary industry (manufacturing industries) and tertiary industry (service industries, such as teaching and tourism).

Computer Power

Computers have had a tremendous impact on the modern world. The microchip and other computer components are usually made in one factory and then transported to other countries where the computers are assembled. Companies like Compaq Computers manufacture servers, workstations, networking products and PCs. Their products are sold not only in Britain but are also shipped to many parts of the world. Wealth is generated from business in this country and from **exports**. Selling products abroad helps with the country's balance of payments (the difference between money for exports and the cost of **imports**). Other companies produce software (such as Oracle) and computer businesses like Electronic Data Systems (EDS) provide e-business and IT services to 9000 organisations in 55 countries. EDS and many other computer businesses are multinational companies.

Computers are used for many different tasks and make an important contribution to the economy. Computing jobs include an archivist (who preserves, retrieves and stores records on a computer system), database administrator (who organises, manages and is responsible for data held electronically), desktop publishing operator, information officer, software engineer, systems administrator (who looks after the day-to-day running of the computer system), systems analyst (who designs computer systems to handle business requirements), web designer and word processor operator. Thousands are now employed in the computer industry, generating wealth for their companies, their families and themselves, their communities (through all the things that they purchase) and the country (through taxes and exports).

For his work experience placement, Ian wanted to explore the impact that computers are making for those who wish to work from home. He secured a place at Barns Designs Internet Services, a small

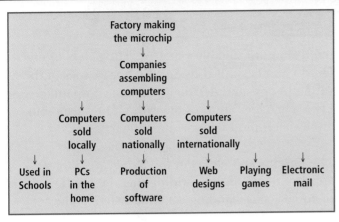

```
              Factory making
              the microchip
                    ↓
               Companies
               assembling
               computers
                    ↓
        ↓          ↓          ↓
   Computers   Computers   Computers
     sold        sold        sold
    locally    nationally  internationally
      ↓          ↓          ↓        ↓        ↓         ↓
  Used in    PCs      Production   Web    Playing  Electronic
  Schools    in the       of      designs  games     mail
             home      software
```

▲ The 'ripple effect' of computers.

local business that was established in 1995 and is based in a home in the North Devon countryside. There he learned how to use some of the latest software to create an eye-catching website for his secondary school. Barns Designs' aim is to make other companies' internet experience as rewarding and profitable as possible and to maximise the e-commerce and internet business potential. This family business works with a small number of companies who complement their range of services with their own. By cooperating they are able to provide additional services, such as website hosting, IT and internet training for a complete business solution, and this leads to more contacts, customers and more business opportunities.

Marketing on the internet is a rapidly growing area of the economy and its advantage is that:

- Millions of people use the internet daily.
- Global coverage is given to the products or services.
- It is the fastest-growing and most cost-effective advertising medium available.

Another important area where a great deal of money is generated is in using computers for entertainment. Whether it is for PCs or PlayStations, millions of pounds are spent in purchasing games, ranging from car races to versions of *Star Wars*.

One company producing commercial games is Criterion Software, which was founded in 1993 and has its headquarters in Guildford, Surrey. Over 160 employees are involved in its software technology and game development divisions, and it has offices in Tokyo (Japan), Austin (Texas, USA), Paris

(France) and Derby. The company is divided into two divisions:

1. Criterion Software which develops, markets and sells 'middleware' technology. These are the tools and technology used by companies all around the world to make their computer games.
2. Criterion Games which develops video games for the major consoles, including Sony PlayStation2, Nintendo Gamecube and Microsoft's X-box.

The company comes up with the idea, designs the gameplay, the characters and levels and then produces the art, writes the code and produces the sound and music. The game is tested and solutions are found for any bugs that are discovered. The process usually takes from 18 months to two years, and then the company delivers a set of gold disks to the publisher, such as Sony or Acclaim. The publisher then produces hundreds of thousands of disks, packages them with a manual and sells them to a distributor. The distributor sells them to a shop or retail chain and the game is marketed worldwide. An after-sales service is provided by the company, which includes specialist advice and support for those having difficulty, and listening to feedback and suggestions. New ideas may result from some of the suggestions, which are vitally important because companies have to keep ahead of their competitors if they are to be successful.

GLOSSARY

Exports: Goods sold to other countries.

Imports: Buying goods from another country.

? Questions

1. Why is a strong economy important for a country?
2. Explain how and why computers have an important impact on the economy.
3. What advantages are there for firms to cooperate in their business operations?
4. Explain how the internet has opened up worldwide markets.
5. What does 'keeping ahead of competitors' mean? Why is this important?

Ethnic Groups

KEY ISSUES

○ How ethnic identity, religion and culture can cause challenges within communities.

It is not always easy living in a community where you are in an **ethnic minority**. Sometimes there are tensions between different ethnic groups. Occasionally these stresses boil over into violence and riots. During 2001 pitched battles took place in Bradford between hundreds of police officers and about 200 rioters, many of whom were young Asian men. Police in riot gear where bombarded by bottles, bricks and petrol bombs and over 100 officers were injured. There were stabbings and 36 people were arrested, including 13 Asians. The disturbances spread to communities in Oldham, Greater Manchester and Burnley in Lancashire, and there were more than 150 arrests. Many believe the riots were in response to activities by the National Front and the British National Party who are opposed to immigrants coming to Britain.

A government housing minister was reported as saying that council housing policies had contributed to the unrest. Lord Falconer said:

'*Black and minority ethnic communities frequently end up in the worst council estates. That's if they can access social housing at all. In Bradford just 2 per cent of council tenants are Asian. Accessing registered social landlords is also difficult … Our vision is that people from all ethnic groups have equal opportunity to access housing and receive quality services. We are a long way from that at the moment.*'
The Guardian, Thursday 26 July, 2001.

What has caused some of the ethnic minorities in Bradford to riot?

Arranged or Assisted Marriages

In some ethnic groups, arranged marriages are the norm. The elders in the family choose partners for the younger generation. They consider the social, financial and religious status of both families to find out if they are suitably matched. The elders of the Hindu families will consider the horoscopes of the young people and decide if they are compatible. Love marriages are possible within Hinduism, but are less common than arranged marriages.

The parents and elders in the family are likely to approve the choice, providing that the families are of equal social standing. In Hinduism it is the custom to live in extended families – three or four generations living together. In her new home, the bride is expected to look after her parents-in-law and other members of the groom's family.

Parents in the Muslim communities often arrange the selection of a marriage partner. Muslims emphasise chastity and modesty and so young people of the opposite sex are not encouraged to spend time together. In such a situation it is difficult for love to come before marriage.

Richard is a member of the lower sixth and he really likes Taiyba. Every time she walks in the room his face lights up and he believes that she has feelings for him. He talks to her at every opportunity and he would love to take her out. She is a British Asian and her family are Hindu. When Richard did ask her to go to a club with him, she politely replied that it was impossible. Richard is even more disappointed when

▲ In many cultures marriages are traditionally arranged.

Taiyba says that her family would not allow her to have a date with him and that they would be choosing her future partner.

Different Customs and Religions

Some members of ethnic minorities in Britain speak very little English, have different customs and belong to communities that follow religions other than Christianity. As a result they can find it difficult to mix with members of the community who speak another language and who have different beliefs. Their holy days and festivals are often different to public holidays and rest-days in Britain. For example, the Muslim holy day of Friday is a normal working day in this country. This causes problems regarding employment, and in Muslim communities the shops are closed on Fridays. During Ramadan, Muslims fast for a month during daylight hours. This can cause them to find it difficult to keep up if they are employed to do manual work by non-Muslims. Festivals such as *Eid-ul-Fitr* may also fall on a working day and so the employee may not be able to get time off to enjoy the celebrations with their family.

The food laws of some religious groups require special shops. Jewish rules and regulations mean that the Jewish communities require food shops selling only kosher food, and the Islamic communities need halal butchers. Muslim meat has to come from animals slaughtered in the name of Allah, and both Muslims and Jews are not allowed to eat pig meat. These rules and other regulations are obstacles to members of these religious groups mixing with other members of society.

GLOSSARY

Ethnic minorities: A group of people who are different to the main population because of their racial origin or cultural background.

? Questions

1 Explain the challenges that immigrants face when settling into a new country.
2 What is meant by:
a) An arranged marriage
b) A love marriage?
3 Should young people only marry within their own culture and religion?
4 Explain some of the ways that religion affects community life.

◄ Riots due to racial tension in Bradford, 2001.

Ethnic Groups

KEY ISSUES

○ How do ethnic identity, religion and culture enrich community life?

Ethnic Communities

The different ethnic minorities have brought many of their customs, culture and celebrations to Britain. This has added colour and variety to community life in Britain. The Queen included the following statement in her message to celebrate diversity in our society and that of the Commonwealth:

'We recognise that promoting diversity is not just tolerating difference. Living together as neighbours needs more than that. The true celebration of diversity involves reaching out, recognising and embracing difference, and in so doing enriching our lives. It requires respect for others and a readiness to learn from them, recognising that we have duties as well as rights; and seeking to leave the world a better place than the one we inherited.'

Elizabeth R., 11 March 2002.

▲ The Chinese Lion Dance at the Bun Festival.

Chinese New Year. The date of the New Year is set by the lunar calendar and varies from late January to the middle of February. The Spring Festival celebrates the earth coming back to life, and the start of ploughing and sowing.

The Chinese community clean their homes, repay debts, cut their hair and buy new clothes. Texts seeking good luck are written on red paper and decorate the doors of their houses, colourful lanterns decorate the rooms and charms are hung up to keep away ghosts and evil spirits. Incense is burned in homes and temples as a mark of respect to ancestors. On New Year's Eve a large family dinner is served and the houses are brightly lit. At midnight, fireworks go off to drive away evil spirits. New Year's Day is often spent visiting neighbours, family and friends.

Celebrations take place on the streets with members from all communities taking part in the festivities. In the major cities like Manchester, Liverpool, Birmingham and London, Chinatown becomes something of a Chinese bazaar, with stalls selling paper dragons, Chinese toys, personalised Chinese calligraphy, Chinese porcelain and Chinese food. Firecrackers are lit and Chinese dragons are paraded in the streets with drums and gongs beating.

Each year crowds of people sample Chinese culture through a number of events such as tai chi demonstrations, Chinese stalls and food.

▲ Prince Charles celebrates a Muslim festival with young people from the British Islamic community.

Chinese New Year

The Chinese Spring Festival is one of the most colourful celebrations and is known in Britain as the

▲ Celebrating at the Notting Hill Carnival.

The Notting Hill Carnival

The Notting Hill Carnival began in London 36 years ago as a result of West Indian immigrants moving into the area. This three-day carnival takes place each August Bank Holiday weekend. The festival was initiated by the black community (particularly immigrants from Trinidad where the Carnival tradition is very strong) and local people who dreamed of creating a festival to bring together the people of Notting Hill. Today the carnival celebrates the diverse cultures that make up multicultural Britain and is attended by up to 2 million people. The authorities often refer to it as the biggest carnival outside Rio, and it is chaotic, noisy and colourful with 40,000 masqueraders parading through the biggest street party in Europe. People in many parts of the world marvel at how people of different cultures and backgrounds party and mix together. Colourful costumes and the commercial floats are spectacles in themselves, but many think it is the music that makes it special. Music at the carnival comes from sound systems playing Soca and Reggae with steel bands and Calypso. People dress in masquerade or 'mas'. Food and drink, including jerk chicken, sweet corn and pig's trotters, can be obtained from the stalls that line the streets. Many are concerned that the carnival has really outgrown the venue as it has evolved into a huge multicultural arts festival.

Practising Faith

Much of the ethnic minorities' community life centres on their beliefs and their places of worship. For example, the *gurdwara* is not only where Sikhs worship but it is also regarded as a community centre. Often language classes are held there so that young people can learn to read and write Punjabi (the home language of many Sikh families) and the language of the Guru Granth Sahib (the Sikh scriptures). Frequently, mother and toddler groups and lunch clubs for senior citizens are held at the gurdwara. After their service, worshippers gather for *langar*, the community meal prepared in the community kitchen. By worshipping and eating together, the Sikh community share each other's problems and give each other support. At the same time they are demonstrating their belief that all people are equal.

The closeness of ethnic groups has allowed customs and traditions to survive for hundreds of years in foreign countries. A Jewish state ceased to exist for nearly 2000 years, but their religion and way of life was kept alive in the communities where Jews lived. Since 1948, thousands have returned to Israel to continue their traditions in the country they regard as their homeland.

? Questions

1 Study the Queen's message. What does she say about the benefits of diversity or variety within our community life?
2 How can we show respect for people with other beliefs and cultures?
3 Explain why celebrations such as the Chinese New Year and the Notting Hill Carnival can help to bring tolerance and understanding between different ethnic communities.
4 Explain why members of religious minorities often live in close-knit communities.
5 'Britain has become a much more colourful and interesting society because of the influence of ethnic and religious minorities.' Do you agree? Give reasons for your opinion.

Ethnic Groups

KEY ISSUES

○ How is power and authority exercised at local level?
○ What are the functions and types of local government?

ⓘ INFO BOX

TYPES OF LOCAL AUTHORITY

In England there are three main types.

- A two-tier system of county and district councils. In some areas there are town or parish councils as well.
- A single-tier (**unitary**) authority. These have replaced the county and district councils in some areas. Forty-six unitary authorities have been created since 1998.
- A single-tier system in the metropolitan areas. There are 36 metropolitan authorities including the Greater London Authority.

   Wales and Scotland have unitary authorities. Altogether there are over 460 principal local authorities in the United Kingdom, but their size varies enormously. For example, Hampshire County Council is the main local authority for over 1.5 million people, whereas the Corporation of London is responsible for just over 4000 people.

Imagine arriving in a community where there was no one to make sure that people obeyed the law. What if there was no one to help look after the elderly and sick, or keep the environment clean and safe? What if people put up buildings wherever they wished in any way they wanted? Imagine a town without the refuse being collected, the potholes in the roads not being mended, without any schools or libraries or car parks. We depend on the government to ensure that these things do not happen, but each community is different. Some communities are urban, others rural, some are in coastal areas, others have a large industrial base, yet others may have specific problems. Things that are important in one area might not be relevant to another town or region. That is why local government exists, because people from the area are able to identify the specific needs of the local community and its people.

The trend is for the creation of single-tier authorities. This is less confusing for the general public because one authority then deals with all the services. With more tiers of government it is not always easy to know which council deals with each particular service. This is particularly the case when there appears to be overlap between the different authorities. Others argue that single-tier authorities are too big and less notice is taken of local people's opinions.

The councils exist to serve the local community, but the real power is with parliament (see pages 38–41), which provides the legislation that determines what the local authorities are able to do. Some things are 'obligatory' which means that the councils have to do them, for example, maintain the public highways and deal with planning applications.

Some services are 'permissive' or allowed, such as supporting the arts in the local area. The main government department that oversees and has responsibility for the local authorities in England is the Department of Transport, Local Government and the Regions (DTLR).

▲ Refuse collection is just one service the Council provides.

ℹ️ INFO BOX

THE POWERS AND DUTIES OF THE COUNCILS

The Local Government Act 2000 made it a duty for local authorities to produce a 'community strategy' for promoting or improving the economic, social and environmental well-being of their areas. In addition, the main duties of the local authorities are as follows.

County Councils

The duties of the county councils include looking after education, highways, libraries, social services, strategic planning, trading standards and waste disposal in their areas. Most also promote tourism and try to attract business to their region.

District/Borough Councils

These councils are involved with building regulations, environmental health, housing, museums, local planning and waste collection. Most promote recreational and leisure facilities and tourism, and provide car parking.

Town/Parish Councils

Towns and parish councils provide allotments, burial grounds, bus shelters, community centres, litter bins, public conveniences, parking, recreational facilities, and war memorials etc. They have the right to be notified of planning applications.

The largest metropolitan authority is the Greater London Authority (GLA). The GLA is made up of a directly elected mayor and a separate directly elected assembly. The mayor and assembly has responsibility for:

- Culture, media and sport.
- Economic development and regeneration (through the London Development Agency).
- Environment.
- Fire and emergency planning.
- Integrated transport system, e.g. the GLA is able to charge motorists a fee for taking their car into the centre of London to encourage the use of public transport.
- Planning.
- Police (through the Police Authority).
- Promoting the health of Londoners.

▲ Ken Livingstone campaigning to become Mayor of London in 2000.

❓ Questions

1. Explain some of the benefits of local authorities being responsible for important services in the local communities.
2. What are the main types of local authority in England?
3. Explain some of the duties of the different types of councils.
4. What are the advantages and disadvantages of single-tier authorities compared to two-tier authorities?

GLOSSARY

Unitary authorities: Single-tier local government that performs all the duties of the county and district councils.

KEY ISSUES

○ How are the local authorities financed?
○ How do the councils work?
○ Should there be regional assemblies for England?

Big Spenders

Local authorities (councils) spend an enormous amount of money – in the region of £70 billion each year. This is money that is obtained through:

- Tax paid initially to the government and then given to the local authorities. This money from central government is known as the revenue support grant.
- Non-domestic rates which is a national tax on business premises.
- Money that is collected through council tax. This is a tax on people's homes and is based on a house's value.
- Money generated as revenue (fees and charges) from the services that local authorities provide.

Councils spend approximately one-quarter of all the money on public services and employ over 2 million people to provide services and carry out their duties. After several preparatory meetings, the full council usually meets in February for a special meeting to agree the budget for the next 12 months and to set the council tax.

Who Runs the Councils?

The councils are run by paid officers and elected councillors. The council officers are appointed by the councillors to oversee the everyday running of the council and to carry out the major decisions made by the councillors. The most senior member of the council officers is known as the chief executive. Officers prepare reports and agendas for the councillors and often make recommendations for the councillors to consider. The councillors can accept, amend or reject the officers' suggestion.

The councillors are members of the community who are elected by voters in their **Ward**. There are more than 20,000 local councillors who represent the electors on the various councils and make important decisions each day that affect the lives of people in the local community.

The council business takes place either in a meeting of the full committee or in committees or sub-committees. The leader of the council is either known as the chairperson, or in some cases they are a mayor of a town or borough. Frequently the chairperson is the leader of the largest group on the council. They usually have a number of civic duties, including entertaining important visitors to the area or representing the council on formal occasions. Other councillors may have special responsibilities, such as chairing one of the committees.

The full council meets in the council chamber and usually sit in a horseshoe shape facing the chairperson of the council. Most councillors belong to a political group and they usually sit in their groups.

In addition to making decisions at meetings, councillors need to monitor and review the effectiveness of the council services and to take action to improve the council's performance when things are not going as well as they should. Constituents also bring their problems to the councillors and make representation to them on various issues. Some councillors hold 'surgeries' where residents can make appointments to see them about matters that concern them. The councillor's job also includes visiting or telephoning constituents, and then speaking or writing to council officials to try to get problems sorted. Also councillors may attend other meetings to represent the council or their constituents, or to find out information to assist them in their job.

▲ Setting the annual local authority budget.

Regional Assemblies?

Scotland has its parliament, Wales and London their assemblies. What about the rest of England? Some argue for English regional **devolution** because the Westminster Parliament is overworked. Following devolution in Scotland and Wales and the setting up of the Greater London Authority, the government has created eight English regional development agencies which have the task of improving the regional economies. These are based in the north-east, north-west, west midlands, east midlands, south-east, south-west and in the eastern region. Will eight directly elected regional assemblies follow? Such a move might necessitate another round of local government reform to create single-tier authorities in England (similar to those in Scotland and Wales), abolishing the county councils. Some argue that regional assemblies would be able to lobby the government and the European Union more strongly than individual councils. This might enable regions to benefit in many ways, for instance by obtaining more grants. Others say that it is unnecessary and would be very expensive to run because it would require more local authority offices and officers.

GLOSSARY

Devolution: The transference of power from central government at Westminster to the regions in order to give local people a bigger say in decisions that affect their areas.

Wards: Councillors represent the residents of an area of the local authority and are elected by and are accountable to the electors of that ward.

? Questions

1 Explain how local authorities obtain the funds necessary to provide services for the community.
2 Explain the role of:
   a) The local government officers.
   b) The councillors.
3 Who do you think has the most power and authority on the councils?
4 *'The citizens of Scotland and Wales have more say in their government, it is about time England had regional assemblies.'* To what extent do you agree? Give reasons for your opinion.

◄ State opening of the Scottish Parliament 1999.

KEY ISSUES

○ How does the democratic process work?
○ How does a person become a councillor?

Standing for Election

One way of bringing about change is to become an elected representative of the people in your area. As an elected councillor, people are able to exert an influence on the decisions that are taken by the local government.

'… democratic election gives local councillors, like Members of Parliament, a special status in public life … It is not a easy task being a local councillor … Certainly no councillor would seek election in order to get rich … but the ambition to serve on a council remains an honourable calling and should be recognised as such.'

Lord Nolan's Report on Standards of Conduct in Local Government.

It is important that a candidate for election is a person of honesty and integrity. Councillors have a responsibility to serve the public interest. It would be improper to use the position to gain financial benefits for him or herself or for family or friends. Decisions need to be made on merit and not because a family friend has tendered for a council contract. To accept a bribe or award a contract as a favour would be an act of corruption and councillors are accountable to the electorate for their actions.

Councillors are elected to serve their constituents for four years. In some authorities, elections are held every year with one-third of the seats being contested at each election. In other authorities, all the councillors are elected at the same time every fourth year. The elections usually take place on the first Thursday of May. If a councillor resigns, moves away from the area or dies, a **by-election** will occur and a person is elected to fill the vacancy. This person will serve until the next election is due to take place and they may seek re-election at that time.

Councillors have a duty to uphold the law and act in accordance with the trust that has been placed in them. It is important for them to help ensure that the council does not waste money and that the right

decisions are made. Leadership qualities, and the ability to be persuasive and to communicate opinions are important because councillors often have to lead campaigns to get things changed.

Councillors who fail to listen to their electors or do not work hard for their areas are likely to lose their seats to another candidate when the elections are held.

INFO BOX

You can become a councillor if you:
- Are 21 or over on the day of nomination.
- Do not have criminal convictions.
- Have property in or work connections with the council area.
- Are a UK, Commonwealth or EU citizen.
- Have not been declared bankrupt.
- Do not work for the council for whom you wish to be a councillor.

Most candidates stand for election with the backing of a political party, for example, Conservative, Green, Labour or Liberal Democrat. Those who do not are known as Independents. Candidates seeking election need a platform or manifesto so that the electors know what they stand for.

Seeking Election

Candidates have to be nominated by electors in the ward. Nomination papers are signed and given to the returning officer by the required date and then

▲ A candidate canvassing for support.

a list of candidates is published. Campaigning takes place during the lead up to the election. This involves each candidate and their election agent producing one or more leaflets, which are delivered to the electors. These leaflets give personal details about the candidates, such as their experience and involvement in community life and the reasons they are seeking election. Electors need to know the policies the candidates have on the key campaign issues. Sometimes public meetings are held so that debates on the issues can take place and electors can put their questions and concerns to the candidates. Candidates and their supporters will canvass support by calling on prospective voters. Their aim is to try to persuade the electors to give them their support on polling day.

Each elector has their name published on the **electoral register** and they are sent a polling card prior to the election to inform them of the location of their polling-station. On the day of the election,

voters visit the polling station and are given a ballot paper. In the polling booth (an area set up so that people can vote in secret), electors put a cross against the candidate or candidates (if there is more than one vacancy) and place the completed ballot paper in the ballot box. At the end of the election, the ballot boxes are sealed and taken to the count for checking. After the papers are counted the returning officer announces the result. In England the 'first past the post system' is used for most elections, which means that the candidate with the highest number of votes is declared the winner.

If an elector is aware in advance that they will not be able to vote in person on the day of the election, they may apply for a postal or proxy vote. With a postal vote the elector is issued with a ballot paper prior to the election and they post their vote to the returning officer. With a proxy vote a person is authorised to vote on someone else's behalf.

GLOSSARY

By-election: An election to fill a vacancy caused by the death or resignation of the councillor or MP.

Electoral register: A list of those who are entitled to vote.

? Questions

1 Why might a person wish to stand for election to the local authority?
2 What qualities do you think it is important for a candidate to possess?
3 How does a person become a councillor?
4 Describe what happens in an election campaign.

◀ Primary schools are sometimes used as polling stations.

How Can Individuals Bring About Change?

KEY ISSUES

○ What actions can individuals take to get things done?
○ What contributions do pressure groups and the volunteer sector make?

Getting Things Done

If you lived in a council house and it needed some repairs, or if you are having a problem with the council estate, what could you do? Council tenants have rights that are laid down in the tenant's charter, which include getting certain urgent repairs done quickly and at no charge. Imagine that it is a problem with the condition of the sink, bath, toilet and other repairs. What could be done?

Step One. Contact the local housing office and explain the problem. Hopefully this will result in the problem being dealt with, but if this is not successful you could use the council's complaints procedure.

Step Two. If step one fails, another avenue is to speak to the local councillor and ask for his or her help and advice.

Step Three. If the situation is not resolved then it is possible to contact your local Member of Parliament or the local government **ombudsman**.

Step Four. In the rare event that the problem is not sorted out, then it might be necessary to seek legal advice.

If the problem concerns the behaviour of the neighbours, you are able to complain to the council whether or not they are council tenants. It may be easier for the council to take action if they are council tenants, for instance, in the worse case scenario the neighbours might be evicted if they are found guilty of using the council house for immoral or illegal purposes.

What Can Individuals Do?

'*Healthy democracies need well-informed citizens who take an active interest in their community. They need people who value themselves and others and are aware of the contribution they can make to society.*'

The Citizenship Foundation, 2001.

It is not just councillors that can be instrumental in bringing about change in society. Individuals can influence local or national government and those with power and authority. There are many legitimate ways that can be used to convince the authorities that change is needed. For example, those who wish to persuade society to take the issue of caring for the environment more seriously could:

• Try to influence schools to educate people about the dangers of exploitation.
• Try to persuade governments to warn and advise people.
• Take part in, or organise, protests against pollution, deforestation and acid rain etc.

Set an example by:
• Using 'green' products, e.g. unleaded petrol or cycling or walking when possible.
• Recycling waste, e.g. paper, glass, metals.
• Encouraging organic farming rather than using too many pesticides.
• Being less greedy, settling for a simpler lifestyle and being less materialistic.
• Writing to MPs, councillors or the media.
• Joining political or pressure groups, e.g. CND or Greenpeace.

There is no guarantee that a campaign for a particular cause will be successful. Many people may not agree or listen to the arguments given. It may not be an issue for them or they may not care.

Pressure Groups and Voluntary Organisations

Many people have personal experiences or very strong feelings, which inspire them to take action on behalf of a particular cause. For example, the successful campaign for gun control gained a great deal of support because of the events at Dunblane. There, a gunman shot and killed schoolchildren and people were determined to try to prevent this sort of tragic event happening again.

Others may campaign to stop the council closing an old people's home or to promote the building of sporting facilities for areas that lack them. Like-minded people often get together to form voluntary groups to promote their cause or to protect their rights, for example, residents association.

Some groups have grown to become national or even international pressure groups such as Campaign for Nuclear Disarmament (CND), National Abortion Campaign, the Society for the Protection of the Unborn Child (SPUC) and Amnesty International. For instance, from a small group of volunteers in a little office in London, Amnesty International has now become the world's largest international **voluntary organisation** campaigning for human rights.

It is said that more people belong to voluntary organisations than work in Britain's farming and clothing industries combined. England has in the region of 200,000 different voluntary organisations. Many of these are charities that raise money for good causes and in 1999 their income was over £13 billion. The National Centre for Volunteering (NCV) estimated that in 1991, 21 million people in the UK took part in one or more voluntary activity, giving more than 85 million hours per week to their chosen cause.

The voluntary sector organisations focus on one or more of the following:
- Support for groups of people who have a common need or interest.
- Campaigning for a cause or group.
- Providing a service in response to a social need.
- Working with other voluntary groups.

Shelter

GLOSSARY

Ombudsman: A government-appointed official who investigates complaints from the public. A number of public services are covered by this system, i.e. National Health Service, local government, parliament.

Pressure Groups: Voluntary groups of people which campaign in regard to a specific issue, e.g. Shelter (Housing).

Voluntary organisations: Groups of people who give up their time to work together on a shared interest, normally for the benefit of others.

▲ Esther Rantzen became President of the Association of Young People with ME after her daughter began suffering from the disease.

? Questions

1 What steps can be taken if an individual wishes the council to take action?
2 Explain, using an example, how an individual can campaign responsibly for the cause of their choice.
3 *'Trying to change things is a waste of time.'* How far do you agree with this statement?
4 Describe the work of pressure groups and voluntary organisations.
5 Why do you think so many people take part in voluntary work?

Vote for Me!

KEY ISSUES

○ How does a citizen participate in the political process?

○ Is apathy (lack of interest or activity among voters) good or bad for politics?

 Which of the two accounts below do you think tells the real story of the 2001 General Election?

A Landslide

- The 2001 General Election resulted in Labour achieving another massive House of Commons majority.
- The Conservatives gained only one seat in the General Election, and afterwards its Leader, William Hague, resigned.
- The Liberal Democrats increased their national vote from 1997 and gained six parliamentary seats.
- The General Election resulted in only a few seats changing hands.

Apathy Rules OK

- The Labour Party had the lowest share of any winning party for more than a century.
- 17 million voters did not bother to vote.
- The number *not* voting outnumbered the combined Labour and Liberal Democrat national vote.
- The **turnout** nationally was only 59.3%.
- The Royal Society for the Protection of Birds now has more members than all the UK political parties combined!

Why Bother?

Politics and government is about power. People who are aged 18 and over can, by voting, help to win **elections** for the **political party** of their choice. Winning an election gives your chosen party the authority (or mandate as it is known) to put the policies you agree with into practice. At the time of a General Election, political parties publish their ideas and commitments on a wide range of issues such as education, health and law in the form of a manifesto (a booklet that is made widely available).

In the United Kingdom, **parliament** is the supreme law-maker. It cannot be challenged within the UK, it can alter and make new laws as it wishes. All other levels of government exist only if parliament wishes them to continue existing. They can be abolished or their power can be changed by a decision of parliament. In some areas of the affairs of the UK, the rules, directives and laws of the European Union override UK laws when there is a conflict. In a democracy like the UK, people who are aged 18 and over can, through the use of their vote in a General Election, change the government.

▲ The centre of power in the UK?

▼ The results for the General Election held in 2001 – excludes Northern Ireland

	Number of MPs	Net Gains/Losses	Total Vote	% of Vote	Change since 1997
Labour	413	−6	10.7m	42.0	−2.4
Conservative	166	+1	8.4m	32.7	+1.2
Liberal Democrat	52	+6	4.8m	18.8	+1.6
SNP	5	−1	0.46m	1.8	−0.2
PC	4	0	0.19m	0.8	+0.2
Others	1	0	–	–	–
Turnout	25,558,424 (59.3%)				
Swing	1.8% Labour to Conservative				

INFO BOX

WHO CAN VOTE?
All British citizens aged over 18 and not disqualified (see box opposite). Commonwealth and Irish citizens who live in the UK can also vote. In addition, UK citizens living abroad can vote.

INFO BOX

WHO CAN'T VOTE IN A GENERAL ELECTION?
Members of the House of Lords, Royal Family, mental health patients, sentenced prisoners and those convicted of illegal electoral practices. The last major change in voting eligibility took place in 1970 when the age of voting was lowered from 21 to 18 years of age.

In Australia voting is compulsory. You can pay a fine if you fail to vote. In this country you do not have to vote, as is highlighted by the low numbers of people who voted in the 2001 General Election (see the table). Some people have questioned whether it would be a good idea to give the option to vote for none of the candidates on their ballot paper. This is known as 'abstention' and voters do not have this choice at the moment.

When people are asked why they do not vote a range of answers are given:
- They couldn't be bothered.
- It's a waste of time.
- The political parties are all the same.
- You know who is going to win here so it doesn't matter if I vote or not.
- I can't make a difference.
- My vote doesn't count.
- Politicians are only interested in us when there is an election.

Some of the reasons people give to explain why they do not vote tell us a lot about what they think about the political process. They think their views do not count, politicians do not listen, or that they cannot make a difference.

Why do you think people do not bother to vote?
Is it important that people vote?

Already the government has made it easier for people to apply for postal votes, they have experimented with longer voting hours, and are considering using large shops as polling stations as well as using emails, the internet and texting. Should voting be made compulsory? Should people have the right not to vote?

GLOSSARY

Elections: A process whereby electors vote in secret in order to elect members to local authorities, National and Regional Assemblies, parliament or the European parliament. Traditionally in the UK, elections are held on Thursday.

Parliament: Supreme law-making body in the UK, it comprises the House of Commons and the House of Lords and meets at the Palace of Westminster in London.

Political parties: Organised groups of people who believe in a shared set of values and policies about the direction in which they wish society to move. In the UK, the three major parties are the Labour Party, the Conservative and Unionist Party and the Liberal Democrat Party.

Turnout: The number of electors who vote in an election, shown normally as a percentage of the total number of electors who have registered to vote.

Questions

1 What was the result of the 2001 General Election?
2 Why was 'turnout' an issue in the 2001 General Election?
3 How do you think more people could be encouraged to vote?
4 What is the case for and against lowering the voting age to 16 from the present age of 18?

▲ Prime Minister's Question Time. This is a session that takes place every Wednesday when MPs can put questions to the leader of the country.

KEY ISSUES
○ When can you make your vote count?
○ Can individuals make a difference?

Citizens Who Have Made a Difference
Martin Bell
In 1997 Martin Bell, a BBC reporter, felt so angry about the 'corruption of public life in the UK' that he stood for election as an Independent candidate in the General Election against Neil Hamilton, a former Conservative minister, who had been accused of accepting money from a business man. Both the Labour Party and the Liberal Democrats withdrew their candidates from the election campaign. Martin Bell won the seat and represented Tatton as an independent Member of Parliament until 2001.

Dr Richard Taylor
Dr Richard Taylor, a retired medical consultant, was so concerned about the downgrading of Kidderminister Hospital, that he decided to fight the Wyre Forest seat at the 2001 General Election. In 1997 he became Chairman of a campaign group fighting to save the hospital. The group had already won 19 seats on the local council when Dr Taylor decided to stand in the General Election. The Liberal Democrats decided not to put up a candidate for the seat and Dr Taylor was elected by a large majority, beating a member of the government. The table below shows the result.

What Is All This Voting For?
General Elections
A General Election is about the collective results in individual constituencies. There is no national total vote that influences the outcome of the election. The party that wins a majority of the constituency seats forms the government.

▲ Martin Bell and Neil Hamilton face one another on Tatton Common during the 1997 election campaign.

The UK is divided into single member constituencies, and each member of parliament is elected for a constituency. Each constituency has, on average, 65,000 electors.

Unlike in other countries, the timing of a General Election in Britain is decided on by the **Prime Minister**. It must be called within five years of the previous election. According to the rules, if the government loses a vote of no confidence (this is a particular type of vote held in parliament and voted on by Members of Parliament) a General Election must be called. This last happened in 1979. When an individual Member of Parliament dies or resigns a by-election is held. This is when an election for an individual seat is arranged to elect a new MP.

Local Elections
Local elections are normally held in May of a given year and the date is fixed by parliament. Some local authorities are all elected at the same time, others opt for one-third being elected each year. When votes are cast in local elections, voters are choosing councillors to represent them on local issues.

Candidate	Number of votes cast	% of votes cast	Change since 1997 % increase or decrease
Richard Taylor Kidderminster Hospital	28,487	58.1%	
David Lock Labour	10,857	22.1%	−26.7%
Mark Simpson Conservative	9350	19.1%	−17.0%
Jim Millington UKIP	368	0.8%	+0.2
Majority	17,630	35.9%	
Turnout 68%, −7.3% since 1997			

Regional Parliaments and Assemblies

In Scotland, Wales and Northern Ireland a new level of government has recently been established where some of the powers from central government have been devolved. In London a new Greater London Authority has been established, headed by a directly elected Mayor. There are proposals to set up regional assemblies in England. All of these changes occurred after being voted upon in referenda. These new bodies elect their members using **proportional voting systems**, whereby the percentage of votes cast for a party equals the percentage of seats they win.

▲ Exercising your vote

 INFO BOX

HOW WE VOTE

In General Elections citizens vote by placing an X on a ballot paper next to the candidate of their choice. The winner of the election is the candidate with the most votes. They do not have to gain a majority of the votes cast, just one more than the candidate in second place. This system is called **First Past the Post**. Most local elections in the UK use the 'First past the Post' voting system.

In a European Election the voter casts a vote by placing an X against the party of their choice on the ballot paper. The country is divided into multi-member constituencies, often electing seven or more MEPs (Members of European Parliament). The political party decides the order of its candidates on the ballot paper. The seats are awarded according to the percentage of votes a party receives. If the Conservatives won two seats, the first two candidates on their list would be elected; hence the system is called the Regional List system.

GLOSSARY

Devolution: The name given to the transfer of power from central government to the locality. In the UK there are now separate parliaments or assemblies in Scotland, Wales and Northern Ireland. Regional powers have been granted to the Greater London Authority and the Mayor of London.

First Past the Post voting system: Traditionally used in the UK to elect members of local authorities and the House of Commons. Voters place an X against the candidate of their choice. The candidate with the most votes wins; they do not require a majority of the votes cast.

Prime Minister: The head of government in the UK, appointed by the Monarch.

Proportional voting systems: The name given to a range of voting systems used in the UK which link the number of votes cast for a party with the number of seats gained.

European Elections

The election of members of the European parliament is held every four years. The day of the week when electors in each country vote can be different, but across Europe the votes are counted on the same Sunday.

Referenda

This is a single issue vote, that can take place at a local, regional or national level. In the UK, the government does not have to act according to the result of the referenda. In recent years there have been referenda about the Good Friday Agreement (in Northern Ireland), Scottish and Welsh **devolution**, and the London Mayor and Assembly.

? Questions

1 Why do you think that Martin Bell and Richard Taylor won their seats even though they were not members of a major political party?
2 What arguments would you put forward to someone who said, 'I never vote. It's a waste of time'?
3 Why do some people think that the First Past the Post System is unfair?
4 What issues do you think are so important that they need to be decided by a referenda?

Vote for Me!

KEY ISSUES

○ Why are there different types of government in the United Kingdom?
○ Who makes the decisions?

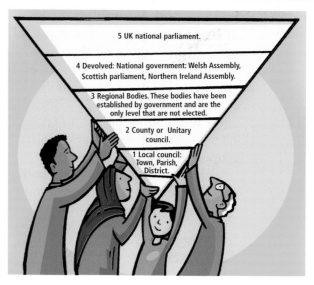

▲ Different levels of government in the UK.

Serving the People

Government within the UK operates at several levels. The term central government refers to the national government of the UK, which is elected every four to five years at a General Election. The parliament of the UK has the power to create or abolish any other type of devolved or local government structure within the UK.

All of us are affected by government decisions and the services that the government provides, either at a local, regional or national level.

Why So Many Levels?

You may be concerned about an abandoned car outside your house, but would you write to the Prime Minister to get it moved?

You may be concerned about the lack of international agreement about the ozone layer, but do you expect your local councillor to resolve this issue?

The services we expect and the power and authority of government are so complex that decisions have been devolved to the appropriate level of government which can then most effectively deliver a service or collect money for local services (through council

taxes). The parliament at Westminster decides the number, structure and powers of all the other levels of government within the UK. Local government or devolved bodies have no automatic right to exist – they are set up by parliament and can be abolished or changed by parliament. In the past, central government has changed the structure numerous times; a Northern Ireland parliament was establish in 1921, abolished in 1972 and re-established in 1998. Local government has seen numerous changes; in 1974, 1986 and 2001–2, its whole internal decision-making process changed to resemble how the **cabinet** works within central government. In most councils a few councillors are each responsible for running a major service and are held accountable to all councillors six or seven times a year. Increasingly, local government is being reorganised into unitary

▲ Parliaments of Wales, Northern Ireland, and the new Greater London Assembly building.

authorities, for example, Plymouth and Bristol, where all the services are provided by one local council.

Who Makes the Decisions?

At a General Election, every four or five years, we cast our votes to elect Members of Parliament (MPs) and after each General Election a new government is formed. MPs receive a salary and allowances for employing staff and running their offices in parliament and in their constituencies

Those elected to the Scottish parliament and the Welsh and Northern Ireland Assembly are full time post-holders and receive an annual salary and allowances for staff, similar to MPs at Westminster.

Local authorities' councillors are part-time and receive an annual allowance. Senior councillors, who are members of the cabinet, receive a larger annual allowance, because their positions are far more time-consuming. A cabinet member responsible for the

education service in your area might be responsible for an annual budget of £300 million and for many thousands of employees.

Town and parish councillors are unpaid and part-time.

i INFO BOX

A recent poll indicated that the average local authority councillor was male, white, aged 55 and retired.

i INFO BOX

STANDING FOR ELECTION
Most people who stand for election are supported by one of the major political parties.
In order to stand for election you need to be over 21 years old.

Once your party has selected you to stand as a candidate, you need to gain the support of some local electors in order to become an official candidate.

In parliamentary and European elections, candidates have to pay a financial deposit which is returned if they achieve a minimum number of votes. For parliamentary elections it is 5 per cent of the votes cast. The amount candidates can spend on their election expenses is limited by law. For local elections it is a few hundred pounds, while it is several thousand pounds for a General Election candidate. National parties spend tens of millions of pounds on national election campaigning.

GLOSSARY

Back bench MP: Name given to any Member of Parliament who is not a government or opposition spokesperson. The name refers to where they can sit in the chamber of the House of Commons, hence the phrase 'front bencher' refers to those who can sit on the government or opposition front row of seats.

Cabinet system: The new local government system of decision making, whereby a few councillors meet and decide how the council should carry out its duties. Each member is responsible for a major local government service. The remaining councillors sit on Scrutiny Committees which monitor the work of the council. Full council meetings, involving all the members, are held several times a year to hold the cabinet to account for its work. The word cabinet is used because the system is based upon the central government model.

Secretary of State: Title given to a senior government minister, e.g. Secretary of State for Northern Ireland.

Shadow spokesperson: An MP from the major opposition party who speaks on behalf of the party on a major policy area and questions the government minister responsible for that area, e.g. Shadow spokesperson for Health. The most important members form the Shadow Cabinet.

? Questions

1 The government is considering introducing regional government for England. What do you think are the advantages and disadvantages of regional government?
2 What are the advantages to us, as citizens, of having a system of local government?
3 Should local councillors be paid a salary like Members of Parliament?
4 Many people say that too many of our politicians have no experience of working outside politics, and do not understand people's problems. Others say that too many MPs are part-time because of their business interests. What would your typical Member of Parliament be like?

KEY ISSUES

○ What are the key structures within the UK system?
○ Who has political power in the UK?

Who Has Power in the UK?

The Monarchy

The **Head of State** is the monarch; the United Kingdom is a constitutional **monarchy**. This is distinct from a republic, like the USA, which has a president who is elected as the Head of State every four years. The power of the monarchy has been reduced over the centuries and now most of its power and authority has been transferred to the government.

The Prime Minister

The prime minister is the leader of the majority party in the House of Commons after a General Election and is the head of government appointed by the monarch. Some presidents are both Head of State and Head of Government, for example, the President of the USA. A prime minister remains in power as long as they retain the support of their own party and/or parliament. Increasingly, prime ministers are accused of being presidential, i.e. acting as a strong leader, rather than as the head of a team that works closely with parliament.

The Cabinet

The cabinet are the leading members of government, appointed by the prime minister, who can also choose to replace them at any time. Each cabinet minister is responsible for running a major government department. The full cabinet meets once a week, but most of its business is done in smaller group committee meetings.

House of Commons

Parliament is the ultimate law-making body within the UK. It is made up of the House of Commons and the House of Lords. Members of Parliament, whom we have elected, sit in the House of Commons. Although the UK parliament makes laws, there are some areas that are governed by European Union law. For example, there are European laws that outline how many hours can be legally worked in a week by people in certain jobs. Parliament has the power to pass legislation – all MPs vote on proposed changes to the law and hold the government, ministers and the prime minister accountable for their actions. In recent years, many believe that the power of parliament and, in particular, the House of Commons, have declined; the power of the prime minister has appeared to increase.

The House of Lords

Parliament also includes a second chamber – the House of Lords. The House of Lords has limited powers and is used mainly to revise legislation that comes from the House of Commons. It also reviews legislation from the **European Union** (EU). Most democratic countries have a two-chamber system in the same way that we have the House of Commons and the House of Lords. The USA has a two-chamber system made up of the Senate and the House of Representatives. The future of the House of Lords is currently being debated. It mainly consists of Life Peers who are appointed for their lifetimes because of their expertise or past political work. It is proposed that instead of all the members

▲ Who has political power in the United Kingdom?

being appointed, some or all should be elected. Some people feel that a largely elected House of Lords would challenge the power of the House of Commons, while others feel an appointed body would be toothless.

The European Union

Since joining the European Economic Community in 1973, now known as the European Union or EU, the UK government has had to share some of its powers and responsibilities with the EU.

The major decisions of the EU are made in the Council of Ministers. This is made up of government ministers from each member country that issue directives and propose legislation, which affect citizens throughout the EU. Regular meetings are held by heads of government of member states, who make major decisions about the future of EU. These bodies meet in secret and are not directly elected by the citizens of Europe. The European parliament, to whom citizens throughout Europe elect members (MEPs), has limited powers, but must be consulted on proposed changes to European law. Its major power is its right to dismiss the European Commission (the cabinet of the EU). The president of the European Commission and the other European commissioners (members of the European cabinet) are nominated by the member governments. The UK has two commissioners. The European parliament almost had to use its powers to dismiss the Commission in 1999 when there were accusations of misuse of power.

So Who Holds Power?

All of these bodies – parliament, the European Union, national, regional and local government – have power over our everyday lives. However, there are others in our society who have power and influence. Today we live in the global economy in an age of mass communication. Many believe that multinationals, the mass media and international financial organisations, such as the IMF (International Monetary Fund) and the WTO (World Trade Organisation) limit the powers of individual countries to make decisions about their futures.

INFO BOX

POWER OF THE EUROPEAN PARLIAMENT EUROPEAN COMMISSION RESIGN EN BLOC

All 20 EU Commissioners resigned in March 1999, following a report into fraud, mismanagement and nepotism. They knew that if they did not resign they would be sacked by the parliament. Some of the things uncovered included:

- A French commissioner appointed her dentist to a senior EU post.
- A Portuguese commissioner appointed his brother-in-law as a key adviser.
- A Spanish commissioner acted slowly when fraud was discovered.

GLOSSARY

The European Union (EU): Currently a union of 15 European countries that are aiming to create a common economic framework. The Union also has a political dimension; some members wish to create a 'United States of Europe' and this is often called Federalism. A large number of former East European countries have applied to join the EU.

Head of State: An elected or appointed person who acts as the chief citizen of a state. Their powers are normally limited by the constitution of the country.

Monarchy: A system whereby the Head of State or monarch owes their position to their historical role as the head of the most important aristocratic family. In the past the monarchy exercised total power over their subjects. Today most countries have constitutional monarchies, where most of their power has been transferred to the elected government. In the UK, the law has recently been amended to allow for the eldest child to succeed to the monarchy, regardless of whether they are male or female.

Questions

1 In the twenty-first century is there a need for a monarchy in the UK?
2 In what ways are prime ministers powerful?
3 How would you reform the current House of Lords?
4 How do you think the European Union could become more democratic?

KEY ISSUES

○ The powers of protest – how far do they go?
○ People power – where it has made a difference.

Getting Involved

Elections only take place every four or five years. How can the citizen influence politicians in between elections? Citizens can bring about change through the ballot, but is that where your democratic rights end? What if you feel that the system does not allow your voice to be heard.

On Your Board!

Paul and Jenny are keen skateboarders and were getting fed up with the constant complaints about their use of the town centre; letters were appearing in the local paper about the skateboarders being a nuisance. They decided to do something about it. They got their fellow skateboarders together and organised a petition to ask the local council if they would provide a site for the skateboarders.

They were invited to a council meeting to put their case and convinced the councillors of the need for a skateboard park. They found a part of a local public park that could be used. A few months later the skateboarders were photographed by the local paper at the opening of the new skateboard park.

▲ Petition leads to skateboard park.

▼ What means of protest do we have as individuals?

At School	In the Community
• Ask questions.	• Join local protest groups.
• Write letters.	• Petitions.
• Petitions.	• Contact local councillors or MPs/MEPs.
• School council.	
• Involve parents and governors.	• Involve the media.
	• Marches/protests.
• Discuss issues with the head teacher or principal.	• Join a political party.
• Involve the media.	

Paul and Jenny achieved what they wanted with the power of peaceful protest by working with their friends and organising a petition. How would you bring about peaceful change in your community?

But what do you do when the society that you live in does not encourage participation, discussion or protest?

The Velvet Revolution

In November 1989 the **one-party**, **communist** system in Czechoslovakia collapsed due to massive public protest. It was replaced by a multi-party system. These events became known as the 'Velvet Revolution' as the change in government took place as a result of peaceful protest by the people.

One of the leaders of the velvet revolution was Vaclav Havel, a leading member of Charter 77, the human rights group set up in 1977 to monitor and fight for human rights in Czechoslovakia. The communists had imprisoned him. After the Velvet Revolution he was elected president of the country. Before 1967 the people of Czechoslovakia had wanted change, but then the Russians sent in their army to crush the reforming communist government and the changes it had introduced. In 1989 the Russians did not get involved in Czechoslovakia or the other countries of Eastern Europe and massive public protest ended communist rule throughout Eastern Europe.

Would You Speak Out?

In Nazi Germany before the Second World War, democracy was replaced by a **totalitarian state**.

▲ People power – Prague 1989.

The law protects many of these means of protest; recently the European Convention of Human Rights was incorporated into UK law. This protects your rights in important areas, for example, a right to a fair trial, freedom of thought and expression, right to free elections and the right to education.

 INFO BOX

What limits should a government place on the rights of individuals to protest? All these are, or have been, in the recent past, illegal in the UK.
- Not to be allowed to join a trade union (GCHQ).
- To drive on a motorway without being asked to turn around during the miners' strike.
- To hold a rave party where you wish.
- To hold a protest march where you wish.

People's freedoms were taken away and individuals lived in fear of arrest or persecution simply because of their religion, political ideas or how much the government thought they were 'worth'.

Pastor Martin Niemoller was an anti-Nazi who was imprisoned in a concentration camp for preaching against the Nazis. He wrote this poem about the Nazis:

First they came for the Jews
And I did not speak out
Because I was not a Jew.
Then they came for the Communists
And I did not speak out
Because I was not a Communist
Then they came for the Trade Unionists
And I did not speak out
Because I was not a trade unionist.
Then they came for me
And there was no one left
To speak out for me.

What rights do you think a citizen should have in regard to the right of protest?

GLOSSARY

Communism: A political and economic system that believes that the state should control all of the political processes and means of production in the state, and that all citizens of the state are equal.

One-party state: A country where only one political party is allowed. There may be elections but there is only a choice between the candidates from one party.

Totalitarian state: Where total power and authority are exercised by the state, which is normally controlled by one political party or group and dominated by a strong leader. There are few, if any, constitutional rights, e.g. Nazi Germany between 1933 and 1945.

 What would you have done?

Your Rights in the United Kingdom
In the UK we believe that the role of government is to protect individual rights, such as freedom of speech or freedom to travel where we want to, and to allow individuals the right of protest and involvement in voting for the party they choose.

? **Questions**

1 How can you, as an individual citizen, make your views heard between elections?
2 Why should some forms of protest be deemed illegal?
3 How are your rights protected in the UK?
4 Are some human rights more important than others?

KEY ISSUES

○ What services does the state provide for its citizens?
○ Should services be provided by the state or the private sector?

Who Should Provide Public Services?

In recent years governments have opted out of providing many services themselves. In the 1980s this was called **privatisation** and allowed services such as water, gas, electricity and telephone to be run by the **private sector**. The government, through a system of regulators and a government-appointed watchdog, still controlled many of the actions, particularly pricing, of these new private businesses, for example, the Office of the Water Industry Regulator (OFWAT).

Providing for the Citizens' Needs

The services provided by local and central government have a direct impact on all of our daily lives.

 What use do you already make of public services and which do you expect to use in the future?

 Do you think there are some government services that should not be run by the private sector?

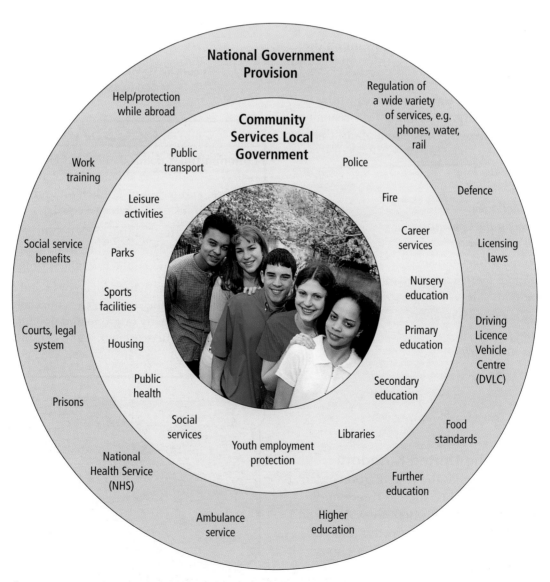

National Government Provision

Community Services Local Government

Help/protection while abroad

Regulation of a wide variety of services, e.g. phones, water, rail

Work training

Public transport

Police

Leisure activities

Fire

Defence

Career services

Social service benefits

Parks

Licensing laws

Nursery education

Sports facilities

Primary education

Driving Licence Vehicle Centre (DVLC)

Courts, legal system

Housing

Secondary education

Public health

Prisons

Social services

Libraries

Food standards

Youth employment protection

National Health Service (NHS)

Further education

Ambulance service

Higher education

▲ The impact of government on the individual citizen.

Increasingly the private business sector will be involved in financing and running aspects of health care, the London underground, schools and building motorways. These schemes are called **private/public partnerships**. The private sector borrows money to invest in these services and sometimes directly manages the service. Many services that are controlled by local and central government have been opened up to private sector competition or the government has converted them into government agencies, for instance, Driving Licence Vehicle Centre (DVLC) in Swansea. These agencies manage their own affairs and budgets, but are still owned by the state and are accountable to government ministers.

INFO BOX

MAKING MONEY OUT OF RUBBISH
How does a private firm make money out of collecting our rubbish? When the council ran the service it was able to work out how much it cost to employ the labour and run the dustcarts. For example, if the local council spent £3.2 million a year to run its own collection service and a private contractor offered to run the same service for £2.7 million a year, the council would save its council taxpayers £500,000 a year. The council pays the private company the £2.7 million and the company then has to provide the service and make a profit.

How do you think the private company makes its profit?

All local councils have to place a wide range of their services out to **tender**. In many local areas the refuse collection is carried out by the private sector because local councils have to find the most cost-effective way of providing the service.

What do you think is the best way to improve the railway system?

Value for Money in Education?
Your school or college is a multi-million pound enterprise, employing a large number of people. The costs of your education are currently met out of national taxation and local council tax.

Do you think the private sector should be involved in running services at your school or college? Think about some of the services that a school uses – school meals, library, computers, careers education, maintenance of the grounds and the buildings.

In the USA, some states are currently introducing education vouchers for individuals to use to pay for their education. Students may use these vouchers at schools and colleges of their choice, public (state) or private (independent) fee-paying institutions. After the student joins the school or college of their choice, the institution cashes in the voucher.

Many believe that 'education vouchers' are the way forward in the UK. What do you think could be the likely impact of them in the UK?

GLOSSARY

Private sector: A term used to describe that part of the economy which is privately owned, mainly businesses that are run for profit and owned by shareholders.

Private/public partnership: A system whereby the private sector and the state jointly run and finance what were formerly state-run services.

Privatisation: A system whereby assets and services owned by the state are sold to the private sector of the economy normally by offering shares for sale.

Tender: A process where one submits a bid or offer to run or provide a service. The lowest priced tender is normally awarded the contract.

? Questions

1 If there were no services provided by local or national government, how would it affect your life?
2 Why does our society have some services provided by the state and others provided by the private sector?
3 What additional services do you think should be provided by the government, and how do you think they should be paid for?
4 What do you think are the key services the government should provide for its citizens?

Picking up the Bill

KEY ISSUES

○ How does the government raise its income?
○ How does the government spend its money?
○ How have citizens reacted to taxation?

Raising the Money

In order to provide public services, the government of any country has to raise revenues.

In the UK, in 2002–3, government spending will be £418 billion. In order to raise this money the government draws upon a wide range of taxes and it borrows money (see pie charts below).

In order to increase the amount of money they spend, governments have to increase taxes or borrow money or both. If the economy is expanding it is also possible for government to maintain or increase public spending and decrease taxation at the same time.

As individuals we contribute to government revenues mainly by **direct** and **indirect taxation**. Direct taxes are those that come directly from your wages, for example, income tax and National Insurance. Indirect taxes are paid on goods or services you use, Value Added Tax (VAT) and **excise duties**, tobacco duty, beer and spirits duty, car tax, and petrol duty. A percentage of all of our VAT is used to finance the European Union.

In recent years governments have cut income tax (direct tax) and compensated by raising indirect taxes, such as VAT and fuel tax. This has meant that those in work have more money to spend, but more of the price we pay for goods or services goes to the government as indirect taxes.

 What impact do you think increasing indirect taxes has on people on fixed or low incomes?

A Tax Too Far

In recent years there have been two major public protests about taxes that have brought change. It is very unusual in this country for citizens to take to the streets about taxation. Most citizens let their views be known when they next have a chance to vote.

Getting Rid of Poll Tax

In 1988–90, the government introduced the Community Charge (Poll Tax) to replace what everyone agreed was the unfair domestic rating system. The new system meant that almost every adult would contribute to the costs of running local councils because the government was concerned that many local councils spent too much and too many people were exempt from paying 'local rates'. Fewer and fewer people were paying more and more to their local councils under the rating system. In addition, the rating system was based upon where you lived and not upon the number of people living in the house. For many people the change to Poll Tax meant a heavy tax increase. The mood of the

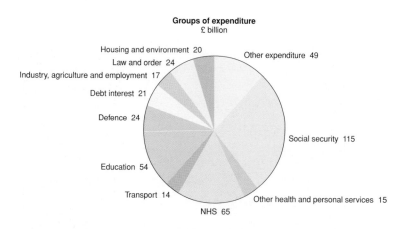

Groups of expenditure
£ billion

Housing and environment 20
Law and order 24
Industry, agriculture and employment 17
Debt interest 21
Defence 24
Education 54
Transport 14
NHS 65
Other health and personal services 15
Social security 115
Other expenditure 49

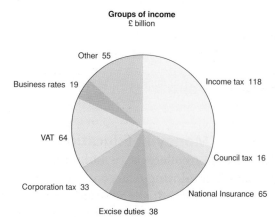

Groups of income
£ billion

Other 55
Business rates 19
VAT 64
Corporation tax 33
Excise duties 38
National Insurance 65
Council tax 16
Income tax 118

▲ Figures taken from HM Treasury 2002/03.

▲ Angry hauliers and farmers protesting about the price of fuel in 2000.

electorate became so anti-Community Charge that numerous protests and demonstrations took place. It was a major contributary factor in the downfall of Margaret Thatcher, the Prime Minister. John Major replaced the Poll Tax in 1990 with a new style Council Tax, which was partly based upon the old rates and the Poll Tax; the public disturbances stopped.

When the Price of Fuel Got Too Much

In 2000, the price of fuel in the UK increased due to a range of factors. These included government taxation policy and the aim of this policy was to encourage the conservation of fuel and lead to the introduction of greener fuels. A group of farmers and haulage contractors felt so strongly about the higher fuel costs that they blockaded an oil refinery; within a few days this became a national protest as more and more refineries were blockaded. The oil tanker drivers who were inside refused to leave the refineries because they were concerned about the danger. Initially the police did little but monitor the situation; increasingly garages were running out of fuel. The public mood was one of support for the protesters. The government was forced to act; what had started as a protest was now threatening to undermine the economy and put lives at risk.

There was a chance that the essential services would run out of fuel – the police, ambulances the fire service, doctors and nurses would be unable to get around. The government held indirect talks with the protesters and within a few days the protest stopped.

The government later changed the way that the fuel tax operated, and when the protesters tried to stage a further protest it was unsuccessful.

> Was the fuel protest a protest too far? How do you think the fuel companies, the police and the government should have reacted?

ℹ INFO BOX

WHY WERE THE HAULIERS AND FARMERS ANGRY?
UK hauliers complained of competition from foreign hauliers who were able to buy cheaper fuel abroad and could, therefore, undermine the UK hauliers by taking work away from them.

The farmers were angry at the cost of their fuel because much of their income was based upon the European Green Pound (a formula used to work out payments from the EU Common Agricultural Policy to UK farmers). This meant that their incomes were falling and their costs rising.

GLOSSARY

Direct taxes: Taxes that are taken directly from your income or savings, e.g. income tax.

Excise duties: Taxes levied on specific goods, e.g. road fund licence, tobacco, fuel, beers, wines and spirits.

Indirect taxes: Taxes that you pay by using certain services or purchasing goods, e.g. VAT and fuel tax.

? Questions

1 If you had to pay for the government services you used, instead of them being paid for by general taxation, who in society would be the winners and losers?
2 What taxes do you think are fairer – direct or indirect?
3 The rich should pay more income tax! What are the arguments *against* this statement?
4 How would you change the way the government spends and raises its revenue?

How is My Life Affected?

The Long Arm of the Law

KEY ISSUES
○ Why do we needs laws?
○ How are laws made?

◀ The Scales of Justice on top of the Old Bailey, London.

Life Without Laws

In the past you were expected to protect yourself and your property. There was no one to turn to for help. We still use the phrase 'survival of the fittest' to describe the situation where the strongest get what they want. A society that lives without laws is said to be living in a state of **anarchy** (see cartoon below). Imagine that you are that little person in the cartoon today. You are using your state-of-the-art mobile phone, and the 'me want' person corners you and threatens you with violence unless you give them your new phone. What help would you expect to be given? Would you expect:

- Those around to show concern and offer help?
- Someone to contact the police?
- The police to catch the criminal?
- A trial to take place and, if found guilty, would you expect the accused to be punished?

Why Do We Need Laws?

Laws are needed:
- To indicate what is unacceptable behaviour in society.
- To show, by the scale of punishment, how seriously society takes the breaking of its rules.

In order to carry out these broad aims, every society constructs a legal system that states:
- How laws are made and how they can be changed.
- Who is responsible for the enforcement of different types of law.
- How the judicial system determines guilt or innocence.

What would happen if we had the following system?

1 Laws   +   Police, but no courts.
2 Police   +   Courts, but no laws.
3 Law   +   Courts, but no police.

The results would be that:

1 You could be arrested but not found guilty and punished.
2 The police can arrest you for anything they want, and the court could punish you in any way it wanted.
3 People would break the law but nobody would catch them, collect evidence or charge them. There would be nothing for the courts to do.

ⓘ INFO BOX

In 2002, one of the UK senior judges proposed that those convicted of stealing mobile phones from people should receive long prison sentences. A large number of these crimes involve young people as both victims and perpetrators. Recently a young girl was shot in the head, just to steal her mobile phone from her.

 Do you think tougher sentences are the answer to mobile phone theft, when the thieves are usually young people?

ⓘ INFO BOX

WHO MAKES THE LAW?

In the UK legislation is enacted by parliament. A proposal for legislation, called a **Bill**, goes through several stages (or readings) in the Houses of Commons and Lords, before receiving the Royal Assent and becoming a law. The government proposes most laws, but individual MPs can also sponsor Bills as can some other bodies, e.g. local authorities.

Me want

Give it to me

Mine

Rules, Rules and More Rules

Laws affect every aspect of our lives. In a school or college there will be a set of school rules or a code of conduct. Many schools now insist on parents and students signing home/school agreements. While the government passes legislation that affects all of us, other groups and organisations to which you belong have their own set of rules or laws.

If these rules or contracts exist formally and there is a disagreement about them, the law decides who is right.

What other groups or organisations do you know or belong to that have sets of rules or laws?

Case Study

Some years ago a mother would not allow her son to be caned at school for breaking a school rule. The school suspended the student for disobeying the school rule. The case went to court and the parents claimed that the school should not use physical punishment and, therefore, should not have suspended their son. The parents lost the case under UK law, but were given the right to take the case to the European Court of Human Rights. There they won their case. As a signatory of the European Convention on Human Rights, the UK government then banned physical punishment in its schools.

This convention is now part of UK law, passed as the Human Rights Act 1998. Courts in the UK could now decide a similar case.

INFO BOX

HOUSE OF COMMONS
Stages in Passing a New Law
1 First reading. The Bill is formally 'Tabled' and a time fixed for its second reading.
2 Second reading. MPs discuss the major ideas behind the Bill. A vote takes place.
3 If MPs vote in favour the Bill goes to the Committee stage where a group of MPs discuss the Bill in detail and propose changes.
4 Report stage. The House of Commons then considers the proposed changes and can make further changes.
5 Third reading. The Bill is discussed as a whole and a vote is taken.

The same procedure is followed in the House of Lords. The Lords amendments have to go back to the Commons for consideration. The Lords can reject legislation, but it can only delay some Bills for one year. Once accepted, the Bill gets Royal Assent and becomes an **Act** of Parliament: the Law. Some laws are also initiated in the House of Lords.

In many areas of our life new directives and laws are made by the European Union and, if they conflict with UK law, EU takes precedence. By signing the Social Contract of the Maastrict Treaty, many changes have been introduced into our working life, for example, the right for men to have 'paternity leave' (time off work to help with their new born baby).

GLOSSARY

Act: The name given to legislation that has been voted on by the Houses of Commons and Lords when followed by the Royal Assent; it becomes law.

Anarchy: A system that rejects the idea of the state and any state structures, including the government, courts and the police.

Bill: A parliamentary proposal for legislation, i.e. a new law or a change to an existing law. It takes the form of a written document, containing many sections and clauses.

? Questions

1 What would life be like without laws?
2 If you had to design a new set of school or college rules for students, what would you include and who would you consult. Who do you think should agree to them?
3 Do you think we, as citizens, should be more actively involved in shaping the laws of the country?
4 Local councils are able to make proposals for local laws (by-laws). If you could propose ideas for local by-laws, what would they be?

The Long Arm of the Law

KEY ISSUES

○ What are the differences between civil and criminal law?
○ How do the courts differ in the ways they deal with criminal and civil cases?

Is it Civil or is it Criminal?
Spot the Difference!

In the UK, laws fit into one of two categories; criminal law and civil law.

> **Criminal law** – Where an individual breaks the law, as determined by the state. It is enforced by the police and the courts. The state initiates legal action against the accused.
>
> **Civil law** – This involves a dispute between individuals or groups and can involve courts awarding damages (a money pay-out) or forcing someone to change their behaviour, e.g. not to see someone or visit them.

THEFT	DIVORCE	DEBTS
PERJURY	MURDER	BANKRUPTCY
ARGUMENT OVER A WILL	SPEEDING	FORGERY
ROBBERY	DRINK	POSSESSION OF DRUGS

 Which of the cases above is civil and which criminal?

Criminal Law

Criminal law involves the police gathering evidence against an individual and preparing a case. This evidence is then forwarded to the **Crown Prosecution Service (CPS)**, a government body that decides whether there is sufficient evidence in order to prosecute the case. The CPS represents the state at court and puts forward the case against the person accused of breaking the law.

Magistrate's Courts

The vast majority of less serious criminal cases are dealt with by **Magistrate's** Courts. The decision about your guilt or innocence is made by three lay magistrates in most towns and cities. In some large cities stipendiary magistrates, who are legally qualified and full-time paid appointments, assist the lay magistrates. Magistrates can only impose sentences within certain limits, while the Crown Court has more extensive sentencing powers.

If you are found guilty, you can appeal to the Crown Court about your guilt or innocence, or about the punishment given. A Magistrate's Court hears the evidence in most cases, initially. Where the offences are very serious, for example, murder, the Magistrate's Court determines whether there is sufficient evidence for the case to proceed to a Crown Court for a full hearing. Magistrate's Courts also deal with licensing laws in relation to pubs, betting shops and casinos.

 Why do you think some people prefer to have their case heard by the Crown Court instead of at a Magistrate's Court?

Crown Courts

Serious crimes are tried in Crown Courts, which were first established in 1972. When an accused person pleads not guilty, a jury of 12 citizens is sworn in to hear the evidence and to reach a verdict. The judge sums up the evidence for the jury and provides legal guidance. Recorders, who are part-time judges, hear less serious cases. Serious cases are heard in front of Circuit Judges who are full-time, and the most serious cases are heard in front of a High Court Judge. Most major cities contain Crown Courts; one of the most famous is the Old Bailey in London. Each Crown Court contains several separate courts because different judges are hearing so many cases at the same time.

ⓘ INFO BOX

MAGISTRATE'S COURT
- Decision made by three lay magistrates.
- Maximum fine £5000 and/or 6 months in prison.

CROWN COURT
- Decision made by a jury of 12 citizens.
- Judge decides the sentence and can give a large fine or longer sentences.

Queens Bench Division
Deals with cases referred by County Court, either due to amount of money involved or on a point of law.

Family Division
Deals with all matters relating to families and personal relationships.

Chancery Division
Deals with tax issues and disputes over wills and large complex financial disputes.

Appeals go to the Civil Division of the Court of Appeal.
Decisions by this court set the way that similar cases are dealt with in the future.

House of Lords
The Law Lords deal with criminal and civil cases referred by the Court of Appeal.
Cases are normally heard by five Law Lords. (Law Lords are senior judges who are made Life Peers.)

Still Think They Got It Wrong?

A convicted person can appeal from the Crown Court to the Criminal Division of the Court of Appeal, and then with the permission of the Court of Appeal, to the House of Lords.

Once all of these appeal procedures have been exhausted and if new evidence is available, a case can be made to the Criminal Cases Review Commission (CCRC) who have the power to refer the case back to the Court of Appeal. Judges hear cases in the Court of Appeal and the House of Lords; no juries are involved.

The Civil Law System
County Courts

If your dispute involves the possible awarding of a small amount of damages, your case is heard in the Small Claims Court. Individuals are offered help and advice by court officials and often present their case. In cases where the dispute involves larger sums of money, repossession of homes, disputes between landlord and tenant and cases involving disputed wills and legacies, divorce and other matrimonial matters, the District or Circuit Judges sitting alone decide the cases.

The High Court

The next stage of courts dealing with civil matters is the High Court. This consists of three separate divisions (see diagram above).

The court system in Scotland differs in its organisation and procedures from the English system.

GLOSSARY

Crown Prosecution Service (CPS): A government body that checks all the evidence put forward by the police and decides whether a case is brought before a court. The CPS then presents the evidence on behalf of the Crown in court.

Magistrates: Ordinary citizens who sit in judgement as members of a bench in a Magistrate's Court, also known as Justices of the Peace (JP). These are part-time appointments which are unpaid and voluntary. Magistrates do receive legal training.

? Questions

1 Would it be better to have more police on-the-spot fines or to clog up the Magistrate's Courts with cases. What are the points for and against?
2 A senior judge proposed that jurors could not deal with some complex cases, and that the decisions are better left to judges. What is the case for maintaining jury trials?
3 What skills and personal qualities would you look for in a lay magistrate?
4 What changes do you think need to be made to the workings of our courts and legal system to make it more accessible to the ordinary citizen?

The Long Arm of the Law

Protecting our Rights from Outside the UK

KEY ISSUES

○ What is the importance of the European Court of Human Rights and the European Court of Justice?

○ What other options are available to the citizen to settle disputes?

European Court of Justice

Two courts outside the UK now need to be considered as part of the UK court system.

After the UK joined the EU, any matters of dispute between member states, or states and the union, are dealt with by the **European Court of Justice**. Its decisions override those of the House of Lords. The court is made up of judges from the member states.

The French government was taken to the court in 2001, over its refusal to allow the import of British beef into France, following the foot and mouth outbreak in Britain. If the French government refuses to lift its ban, the court will impose a fine on the French government. The European Commission took the French to the court for not implementing EU policy. Both individuals and organisations can take cases to the court, providing they deal with issues relating to the European Union.

A group of supermarkets in the UK want to sell ranges of luxury and designer goods in their shops. The manufacturers of these goods refuse to sell to these supermarkets, as they believe their goods, for example, perfumes and clothing, are not suitable to be sold within supermarkets. The supermarkets have had to buy these products on what is called the 'grey market' from other suppliers, and have sold these goods at a large discount. The supermarkets argue that the action of the manufacturers is a barrier to competition.

 If you had to decide about supermarkets selling luxury items, what would be your verdict?

European Court of Human Rights

The **European Court of Human Rights** in Strasbourg was established as a result of the European Convention of Human Rights, which was written by the Council of Europe. This convention lays down basic human rights that must be safeguarded by every state that agrees to the convention. Most countries have written the convention into their nation's laws. The UK, while signing the convention, did not incorporate it into UK law until 1998. Prior to 1998, English courts allowed appeals to the European Court. In 30 years, the UK government has been judged to have violated the convention over 50 times.

The Human Rights Act 1998 formally made the European Convention of Human Rights part of UK law. Now, UK courts can decide cases that appear to contravene the convention and only as a last court of appeal will cases proceed to the court in Strasbourg. The Human Rights Act affects us all.

 How do you think the Human Rights Act will affect you?

Alternative Dispute Resolution

There are other ways of settling disputes that do not involve the formal court system. The government is encouraging citizens to use these other methods because they are less intimidating, sometimes resolving issues more quickly and are often far less costly for the individuals and the state.

If you have a dispute with your employer you may be involved in an Industrial Tribunal. This is a formal hearing where both sides give evidence before a legally qualified chairperson and others representing employer and trade union viewpoints. The decisions of these bodies are binding and normally take the form of a monetary award. Other tribunals deal with issues such as taxes and social security.

▲ The European Court of Human Rights in Strasbourg.

INFO BOX

YOUR EUROPEAN CONVENTION OF HUMAN RIGHTS

- The right to life
  This limits rights for the state to take someone's life.
- Prohibition of torture
  You cannot be tortured or treated in an inhumane or degrading way.
- Prohibition of slave or forced labou
  You cannot be treated as a slave or forced to perform certain kinds of labour.
- Right to liberty and security
  Clear legal procedures to follow regarding arrest and detention.
- Right to a fair trial
  You have the right to a public, fair trial within a reasonable time. In criminal cases you are presumed innocent until proved guilty.
- No punishment without law
  If laws or punishment change you cannot have judgement made against you for something which at the time was not an offence.
- Right to request for private and family life
  Respect for your private life, your home, correspondence and family.
- Freedom of thought, conscience and religion
  You are free to hold a broad range of views.
- Freedom of expression
  You have the right to hold opinions and express your views.
- Freedom of assembly and association
  You have the right to assemble with others in a peaceful way. Also the right to associate with others, e.g. to form a trade union.
- Right to marry
  Men and women have the right to marry and start a family. National laws can still govern how and at what age.
- Protection of property
  You have the right to have the peaceful enjoyment of your property.
- Right to education
  You have the right not to be denied access to the education system.
- Right to free elections
  Election to state bodies must take place by secret ballot and be free and fair. Age or other qualifications can be imposed at a national level.
- Abolition of the death penalty
  The death penalty can only be used in very exceptional circumstances, e.g. war.
- Prohibition of discrimination
  You have the right not to be treated differently on grounds of race, religion, sex, political views or any other status.

INFO BOX

WHAT OPTIONS ARE AVAILABLE TO YOU TO SETTLE A DISPUTE?

- Direct negotiation with the other person or organisation.
- Mediation – using a third party to seek a mutual agreement. This is someone that each side jointly agrees to.
- Ombudsman – an external and independent investigator either set up by the government (e.g. parliament, local government or health service) or by a specific industry (e.g. building trade, consumer credit, financial services, insurance).
- Regulators – established by the government to safeguard consumer interests (e.g. Gas, Water and Electricity.
- Arbitration – a neutral arbitrator considers both sides' evidence and makes a decision which is binding.

GLOSSARY

Alternative dispute resolution: Term now widely used to describe the range of non-court options available to citizens who wish to settle disputes.

European Court of Human Rights: A separate non-EU institution, concerned with the enforcement of the European Convention on Human Rights among citizens of those countries that have signed the convention. The court is based in Strasbrourg.

European Court of Justice: The Court of the European Union (EU) that deals with matters relating to the Treaties of the European Union.

Human Rights Act 1998: The incorporation into UK law of most of the points contained in the European Convention of Human Rights. Acts as a safeguard for basic human rights.

? Questions

1. What is the case for and against the European Court of Justice being able to make decisions about issues in the UK?
2. Once you have studied the Human Rights Convention, what issues do you think are likely to come before the courts to be resolved?
3. If you were in dispute with an organisation that had given you poor service or advice, what options are open to you to resolve the issue?
4. What other **alternative dispute resolutions** would you like to see introduced.

Case Studies

KEY ISSUES

○ How are citizens involved in the legal system?
○ Who does what within the system?

The Law in Action

▲ How could you be involved?

One of a citizen's duties is serving on a jury in a court case. With 11 other citizens chosen at random you have to decide the verdict in a court case. Citizens also, at times, take other roles in the legal process.

Case Study – A Mugging

Darinda and her mother are out shopping when Darinda meets some of her friends. Suddenly a man approaches the group and punches one of Darinda's friends, Alesha, who is using her mobile phone; the man steals the phone and runs off. Alesha is shaken and frightened but unhurt.

Alesha calls the police who quickly arrive on the scene. They take statements from Darinda, her friends and her mother. The group are able to give a good description of the man who stole the phone.

A week later Alesha is asked to visit the police station and she agrees to look at an identity parade. She identifies, from those in the identity parade, the man who stole her phone. The police charge the man with robbery and send all their evidence to the Crown Prosecution Service.

Some weeks later a commital hearing is held in the local Magistrate's Court. The case is heard in front of three magistrates who are advised on legal matters by the **Clerk to the Justices**. The press attend and the case is reported in the local paper.

Due to the serious nature of offence, the magistrates, after hearing the evidence, commit the defendant to the Crown Court for trial. As the defendant is unemployed, he receives Legal Aid to pay for his defence. The magistrates have the power, if they wish, to remand the defendant in custody, keeping him in prison if they feel he will commit further crimes, until the Crown Court trial.

The defendant pleads not guilty to the offence and so a full hearing takes place. At the Crown Court Alesha sits anxiously in the waiting room before giving evidence. The case opens with the **barrister** for the Crown outlining the case. Witnesses are called to give evidence to support the Crown's case.

▲ A Magistrate's court hearing with magistrates, the CPS, a defence solicitor, defendant, the press, Clerk to the Justices, specialists, probation service and social services.

▲ A Crown Court scene with judge, jury, defendant, the press and barristers.

Alesha tells the Court about the robbery. The Crown barrister carefully leads her through her evidence, asking her if she recognises the person who attacked her in court. Alesha points to the defendant.

The judge then invites the barrister for the defendant to cross-examine Alesha. She is very nervous because the barrister challenges a lot of her evidence, in particular, her original description of the robber. Some of Alesha's friends, including Darinda and her mother, are called upon as witnesses and are each cross-examined.

The defendant's barrister calls witnesses to support the defendant's case that he was elsewhere at the time of the offence. These witnesses are cross-examined by the Crown's barrister. After all the witnesses are called, both the Crown and the Defence make closing statements to the court.

The judge, who has listened to all the evidence, points out to the jury the main points of law involved in the case and which particular parts of the evidence need to be closely examined.

The jury retire to consider their verdict. In the jury room they sit and discuss the evidence. The foreperson of the jury asks for people's verdicts – guilty or not guilty. If they do not all agree upon what is called a unanimous verdict, they will discuss the matter further. In this case the jury cannot reach a unanimous verdict. The court meets again and the judge agrees to accept a majority verdict, a maximum of 10 votes to 2. The jury retire and reach a majority verdict.

The court meets again and the jury have decided by 10 votes to 2 that the defendant is guilty. The judge then passes a sentence, bearing in mind any previous convictions of the accused. In this case the defendant has previous convictions for robbery and was sentenced to 12 months in prison.

Any appeal against a Crown Court decision goes to the Criminal Division of the Court of Appeal (see pages 54–55). Often these cases take the form of paper presentations to the Court rather than full formal hearings involving witnesses. Appeal cases are heard before at least two High Court judges and do not involve juries.

GLOSSARY

Barrister: A highly qualified lawyer who specialises in particular aspects of civil or criminal law. Normally represents clients in the Crown Court and High Courts.

Clerk to the Justices: A legally qualified full-time official of the court who provides legal advice to magistrates.

? Questions

1. Some people say that there is no need to have juries in most cases today. What is the case for and against keeping the jury system?
2. Why is it important that the CPS, rather than the police, decide who should be prosecuted?
3. At present the CPS have to reveal all of their evidence to the defence before a trial, but the defence do not have to reveal theirs. Do you think this is right or fair?
4. Is there still a role for the 'unqualified magistrate'? Should all cases be heard by full-time qualified legal experts? What are your views and opinions?

KEY ISSUES

- Do we have a right to privacy?
- The rights of young people.

The Case of the Killers of James Bulger

▲ James disappearing from the shopping centre, caught on CCTV.

Bulger Killers Win Freedom

In June 2001, Jon Venables and Robert Thompson, aged 18, were freed on Life Licences, having spent eight years in secure accommodation for the murder in 1993 of two-year-old James Bulger.

The Unfolding of Events

12 February 1993

James Bulger, aged two years, was abducted from a shopping centre in Bootle. A search was launched to find James. The police were able to use the CCTV footage from the shopping centre to follow James' last known movements. James' battered body was found near a local railway line. Following close examination of the CCTV footage, the police arrested Thompson and Venables. As they were both aged ten, their names were not allowed to be released to the press or the public.

24 November 1993

Thompson and Venables, both aged ten, were convicted of James' murder and unusually named by the judge. They were both sentenced to at least eight years of secure Youth Accommodation. They were to remain in Youth Accomodation rather than prison when they got older.

December 1999

The European Court of Human Rights (ECHR) decided that Thompson and Venables did not receive a fair trial because of the way the court was set up and the way the boys were questioned.

26 October 2000

The **Lord Chief Justice** ruled that the parole process for Thompson and Venables can begin and that they could be free within months. The announcement caused much public opposition, especially in Merseyside.

A Right to Privacy?

The James Bulger murder was committed by two young boys aged ten. When their names were known and when on 22 June 2001 they were released from secure accommodation, they were given new secret identities for their own protection.

Later that same month, the *Manchester Evening News* published information on the whereabouts of Thompson and Venables. The **Attorney General** took the newspaper to court for breaking the **injunction**, which prevents details of the new lives and whereabouts of the two killers being disclosed.

▲ Dame Elizabeth Butler-Sloss.

◄ Protesters outside the Court as Venables and Thompson are driven away.

The case of Venables & Thompson versus Newsgroup Newspapers and others was heard before Dame Elizabeth Butler-Sloss, sitting in the Family Division of the High Court. The case involved the rights of Thompson and Venables to be protected under the Human Rights Act 1998 in regard to the law of confidence. The judge ruled that in the case of these two boys, the right of confidentiality was more important than the right of the media to publish information about them.

The newspaper was fined £30,000 for their contempt of court in breaching the information to protect the 'lives and physical safety' of the murderers of two-year-old James Bulger.

This is a case study of a complex court case. The Attorney General representing the government who first applied for the injunction to give Thompson and Venables privacy from the media, took the newspapers to court for breaking the injunction. This was done in the same way that the local council may take out an injunction against some noisy council tenants and take them to court for breaking the injunction. Or you, as an individual, could take someone to court for failing to pay a bill.

The court in this case was the High Court, Family Division and the judge was a senior High Court judge. Both sides would have been represented by barristers and called witnesses to support their case. The judge alone would decide the outcome of the case. There would be no jury present. In this case a £30,000 fine was imposed. The newspaper could consider an appeal to the House of Lords.

GLOSSARY

Attorney General: Senior law officer of the government.

Claimant: The name given to a person bringing a case against another in a Civil Court.

Injunction: A binding legal direction prohibiting certain actions.

Lord Chief Justice: The most senior judge in England and Wales. Scotland and Northern Ireland have their own Lord Chief Justice.

? Questions

1 What sentence would you have given to Thompson and Venables? Give reasons for your answer.
2 Why do Thompson and Venables need to have new identities and live in secret locations?
3 Do you think that they have a right to privacy?
4 Why do cases such as Thompson and Venables attract so much media attention?

KEY ISSUES
- What can an individual do to fight injustice?
- How can public and media pressure make a difference?

The Case of Stephen Lawrence

▲ Stephen Lawrence.

Going to a solicitors and fighting a case in court can be a very daunting experience; but if you feel the legal system has let you down, what can you do?

On the night of 22 April 1993, Stephen Lawrence, an 18-year-old sixth form student, and his friend Duwayne Brooks were rushing to catch a bus in south-west London. They were confronted by a gang of white youths. They set upon Stephen and Duwayne was chased off by the youths. Stephen broke free but, badly beaten and bleeding after he was stabbed during the assault, he staggered 200 m and then collapsed in a pool of blood and died. It soon became clear that the motive for the murder was racist.

Why Is This Case So Different?
The murder of Stephen Lawrence has led to two police inquiries, a Public Inquiry, and the Macpherson Report.

This case has gained prominence due to a campaign for justice led by Stephen's parents and supporters, who felt let down by the police, the Crown Prosecution Service and the Criminal Justice system. The case almost let to civil unrest; many people felt that the case summed up their views of how the Metropolitan Police operated. The continual inability of the court to deliver what Stephen's supporters felt was justice caused people to feel frustrated and dissatisfied with the legal system.

The campaign by the Lawrence family and their supporters involved the media, politicians and a private prosecution for murder.

What Did the Police Do?
The first person on the scene was an off-duty police officer. The police received numerous tip-offs within hours of the murder, but officers appeared to take a casual approach to the investigation.

The Lawrence family were unhappy about the police investigation and complained. Two internal police inquiries were held. After the first internal inquiry, a senior Scotland Yard officer reported that the case had 'progressed satisfactorily and had been correctly pursued'. The second internal inquiry was ordered by the **Police Complaints Authority** (PCA) and was carried out by the Kent police. This inquiry concluded that the police had been well organised and effective and that there was no evidence of racist conduct. However, with the collapse of the court case, it was clear that the police had bungled their investigation.

The Part Played by the Media
The Lawrence family and their supporters were able to involve the media in their campaign. Following the collapse of the Lawrence's private prosecution, the media began to realise that this case could lead to an explosion in Britain's race relations.

Stephen's parents were interviewed by the *Daily Express.* Nelson Mandela met them. In 1997, the *Daily Mail* devoted its front page to Stephen's case; under the headline 'Murderers' it pictured the five accused. This brought widely different reactions; some congratulated the *Mail* for stepping in where the law had clearly failed; others called it 'Trial by Media'. The *Mail* invited the five to sue for libel. They have not yet take up the offer.

The attitude and behaviour of those accused of Stephen's murder raises issues at the core of our justice system. The police admitted that they had enough evidence to arrest two of the five, but a decision was taken to wait. The police kept a watch on the accuseds' homes, but did not follow them when they left their homes because they did not have mobile phones to call for assistance. At the private prosecution, the jury were directed to acquit the accused despite a secretly shot police video which showed some of the accused using aggressive and racist language.

At the hearing the accused were asked: 'What is your name?' 'I claim privilege … I claim the right to remain silent'. They said the same words repeatedly when questioned. At the Macpherson Inquiry, the five accused showed contempt for the hearing by giving answers such as 'I have no idea' and 'I don't remember'. Outside, civil disorder broke out and as they arrived and left the Inquiry, the accused were pelted with missiles by the crowds.

INFO BOX

WHAT CAN NOW HAPPEN TO THE FIVE?
The three who were acquitted cannot be tried for Stephen's murder again because of the Double Jeopardy rule – no one can be tried for a crime of which they have already been cleared, even if incontrovertible proof of their guilt comes to light (e.g. DNA evidence). What do you think about this?

INFO BOX

THE MACPHERSON REPORT
The main outcomes of the Macpherson Report were:
- A call for reform of the rule of double jeopardy.
- To extend the Race Relations Act to cover the police, armed forces and immigration service. Commission for Racial Equality (CRE) to be allowed to bring legal action against the police.
- To make using racist language a criminal offence.
- An accusation that the Metropolitan Police were **institutionally racist**.
- That prior to trials or inquest hearing, victims should be given advance disclosure of evidence.
- That the National Curriculum in schools should emphasise the value of cultural diversity.

After the Report was published, the Prime Minister, Tony Blair, said 'It will certainly lead to new law but more than that it brings a new era of race relations'. Stephen's parents watched from the gallery of the House of Commons as the Prime Minister praised them in pursuing their son's case.

GLOSSARY

Institutional Racism: A term used in the Macpherson Report to describe attitudes and approaches of organisations in regard to the use of negative stereotypes of ethnic minorities. The Macpherson Report used this term in relation to the Metropolitan Police in London.

Police Complaints Authority: A government-appointed body that independently investigates complaints against the police.

Questions

1 Why is the Stephen Lawrence case so important?
2 Should the law on Double Jeopardy be changed?
3 What do you understand by the phrase 'trial by media'?
4 What changes would you introduce into the police force in relation to training, working in the community and dealing with suspects in order to help improve race relations?

▲ Three of the murder suspects leaving the Court of Inquiry.

How Does the Law Affect Me?

The Right to Live or Die?

> ### KEY ISSUES
>
> ○ Should courts decide life or death issues?
> ○ Human rights – how are they defined?

Pleading for the Right to Die

Case One

'Miss B' is a 43-year-old woman who, because of a ruptured blood vessel in her spine, is unable to move or breathe without the aid of a life-support machine, but she is fully conscious and able to speak. She applied to the High Court to request that her life-support machine be switched off, knowing she would die sometime shortly afterwards. Her doctors had refused to switch off the machine because it was against their professional ethics which state that their duty is to safeguard life.

Miss B gave evidence to the judge, Dame Elizabeth Butler-Sloss, from her hospital bed via a video link to the High Court. Miss B explained that she was aware of the consequences of having her life-support machine switched off, and said 'I want to be able to die'. The judge said that the only issue for the court to decide was whether Miss B had the capacity to make the decision to refuse further treatment. The court also met Miss B in the hospital, around her bedside.

Miss B's chances of any improvement are less than 1 per cent. The doctors said that they could not give an indication of what life could be like for Miss B until a whole range of tests had taken place. She could have the use of a spinal jacket to support her back, a powered wheelchair or artificial arms controlled by her mouth or eyes.

There have been cases in the past where the High Court has allowed doctors to stop supporting the lives of people in a 'persistent vegetative state', with no chance of recovery or quality of life. This case is different in that the patient is mentally alert and able to communicate, and her condition is stable.

In her judgement, Dame Elizabeth Butler-Sloss said Miss B had the 'necessary mental capacity to decide to refuse medical treatment'. The judge gave Miss B the right to transfer to another hospital where her wishes would be carried out.

 Do you think the judgement was correct?

A few weeks after the Court decision, Miss B died peacefully in her sleep after doctors at her new hospital switched off her life support machine.

◀ Miss B's bedside.

Case Two

What do you think the Court should decide?

Diane Pretty was a 43-year-old mother of two who was paralysed from the neck down and unable to talk without the aid of equipment, due to Motor Neurone Disease. This disease is progressive and she had not responded to any treatment. Eventually Diane would die from pneumonia and respiratory failure when her breathing muscles became affected by the disease.

Diane was diagnosed with the disease in 1999 and her condition rapidly deteriorated. Diane wanted to end her life with dignity and needed help from someone to assist her to die. Anyone assisting someone to die is committing a crime. Diane wanted her husband to assist her to die when she wished; but to protect her husband from criminal prosecution she applied to the courts, using clauses of the Human Rights Act.

After a series of court cases Diane Pretty appealed to the House of Lords where her case was rejected. Diane appealed to the European Court of Human Rights, who agreed to hear her case as a matter of urgency.

Diane was supported in her case by the pressure group **Liberty** and the Voluntary Euthanasia Society. Her case was based upon Articles 3 and 8 of the Convention, The Prohibition of Torture or Treatment that is Inhumane or Degrading, and The Right to Respect for Private and Family Life.

On 29 April 2002 the European Court of Human Rights rejected Diane Pretty's appeal. She died from the disease on 11 May 2002.

If you were a judge in the European Court of Human Rights what would be your verdict?

INFO BOX

Motor Neurone Disease affects about seven people in every 100,000. Those afflicted normally die within three to five years and the average age of death is 60. There is no medical treatment.

Extract from *Blacks Medical Dictionary*, 38th edition, 1995.

How does Diane's case differ from that of Miss B?

GLOSSARY

Liberty: A UK-based pressure group that campaigns on human rights and justice issues.

Questions

1. How does the case of Miss B differ from that of Diane Pretty?
2. Why is the Diane Pretty case being heard in the European Court of Human Rights in Strasbourg?
3. How does a civil case differ from a criminal case?
4. a) Why do courts get involved in life and death issues?
   b) Do you think it is right that the law should decide whether or not someone has the right to die? Give reasons for your answers.

▲ Diane Pretty and her husband.

Have I Got News for You?

KEY ISSUES

○ How important is a free press?
○ Is the media just powerful or too powerful?

When you go out to buy a newspaper you have a choice. Can you imagine what it would be like if you had only one newspaper to read and only one TV channel to watch, satellite dishes were banned, and both the newspaper and TV content was decided by the government? Governments have done this because they know the **mass media** has the power to influence people's opinions. The former Taliban government in Afghanistan banned the use of satellite dishes so that people did not have access to information from outside the country.

In this country we expect to have a **free press**, one where choice is not controlled – and the media is not intimidated by the government. We expect our TV channels to be free of political bias. Many people worry that the media is too powerful in influencing public opinion. In particular, there is concern that the press expresses the views of its owners and that, in order to boost circulation or viewers, the media trivialises important issues or sensationalises others. There is a common view that television and especially newspapers, influence the political and social agenda of the country.

Case Study – The People's Princess

On 31 August 1997 in Paris, Diana, Princess of Wales was killed in a car crash. Because Diana was divorced from the Prince of Wales, she no longer had the title Her Royal Highness (HRH), so royal protocol stated that she was no longer a member of the Royal Family. The newspaper and front pages accused the monarchy of not caring and of being out of touch. The Prime Minister, to avoid a crisis of confidence among the public, worked directly with the Palace regarding the monarchy's reaction to Diana's death.

The Prime Minister coined the phrase the 'People's Princess', the flag at Buckingham Palace (against Royal protocol) was lowered and the Queen met the public who had come to grieve and leave flowers.

▲ The death of Diana.

For the first time in her reign, the Queen gave a live television broadcast to express her sorrow about the death of Princess Diana. This was written in consultation with 10 Downing Street.

The death of the Princess of Wales also showed the impact of TV. On the day of her funeral more than 1 million people lined the streets of London, but an estimated 2.5 billion people worldwide watched the live television coverage.

The Power of the Press

In the USA in 1972, the *Washington Post* broke the story of the break-in at the Watergate building, the HQ of the Democratic Party, in the lead up to the Presidential Elections. The newspaper continued to investigate the story, and it eventually linked senior members of the Republican Party and the Republican President Nixon to those responsible for the break-in.

President Nixon resigned from office, rather than be voted out, due to the Watergate affair. He tried to use his powers as president to stop information being made available, but eventually he was forced to release audio tapes of conversations that had taken place in the Oval Office which proved that he knew what was happening.

Gagging the Press

In 1972, the *Sunday Times* wanted to print a story about how thousands of children, born with deformities after inadequate testing of the drug

▲ Nixon makes his farewell speech following his resignation.

Thalidomide, were being offered meagre compensation by the manufacturer. The Attorney General won an injunction that prevented the story being published. The House of Lords upheld the decision, saying that the article would prejudice any legal proceedings. The paper appealed to the European Human Rights Court, which ruled in 1979 that the injunction violated the convention. The scandal led to a Medicines Act about the testing of new drugs.

GLOSSARY

Mass media: Means of communicating with a large number of people at the same time, traditionally associated with newspapers, magazines, radio, television and film.

Free press: The ability of the press to publish stories and information, subject to the same legal safeguards as anyone in society, compared to societies that strictly control the content and the production of newspapers and magazines.

? Questions

1. Why is it important to have a free press?
2. How has the monarchy attempted to improve its media image in recent years?
3. Why are politicians so concerned about their media image?

▲ Too Much News?

Is the Press too Powerful?

> ## KEY ISSUES
>
> ○ Is the press too influential?

Named, Shamed

In July 2000, the *News of the World* published a front page story headlined 'Named, Shamed'.

▲ Paedophiles were named and shamed in the News of the World.

▲ Paedophile protest in Portsmouth, 2000.

The media had been reporting for some time stories about child molesters and paedophiles triggered by recent court cases and the sentences being given. This was particularly prompted by the murder of Sarah Payne aged eight by Roy Whiting, a man who had previously been convicted of kidnapping and serious sexual assault. Whiting had served a prison sentence for these offences. The *News of the World* decided to publish the names of all alleged paedophiles. This led, in some parts of the country, to vigilante groups attacking those named and forcing them to move home. Some people with similar names to those published were also attacked. The police and some rival newspapers attacked the *News of the World*, stating that their action would be counter-productive and could drive the named offenders whose names are on the Register of Sexual Offenders further underground.

The Power to Influence – *The Sun*

Most people are aware that different newspapers have different political views and support different political parties. Throughout the 1980s and early 1990s, a majority of the national press, by circulation, supported the Conservative Party. In 1992, *The Sun* declared 'It was the Sun wot won it' when John Major, the Conservative Prime Minister, won the General Election against the odds.

'It was the Sun wot won it'

On the day of the election, *The Sun*'s front page made its position known:

By 1997 *The Sun* had changed sides and supported Tony Blair and the Labour Party. For the 1997 General Election, the headline was again:

'It was the Sun wot won it'

INFO BOX

HUNGRY FOR NEWS

- On an average day, 60 per cent of people aged 15 and over read a national morning newspaper.
- 70 per cent read a Sunday newspaper.
- There are about 1400 regional and local newspaper titles.

The Impact of the Press

Newspaper Circulation	National Daily Popular Newspapers
Daily Mirror	2,133,996
Daily Star	620,823
The Sun	3,405,343
Daily Express	936,407
The Daily Mail	2,436,375
Source: ABC (Audit Bureau of Circulation), March 2002.	

Newspaper Circulation	National Daily Quality Newspapers
The Daily Telegraph	1,009,499
Financial Times	488,235
The Guardian	406,875
The Independent	227,905
The Times	712,986
Source: ABC, March 2002.	

Newspaper Circulation	National Popular Sunday Newspapers
News of the World	3,983,603
Sunday Mail	687,818
Sunday Mirror	1,796,388
Sunday People	1,352,495
Sunday Sport	196,581
Sunday Express	833,618
The Mail on Sunday	2,352,693
Source: ABC, March 2002.	

Newspaper Circulation	National Quality Sunday Newspapers
Independent on Sunday	236,199
The Observer	456,945
The Sunday Telegraph	797,125
The Sunday Times	1,406,548
Source: ABC, March 2002.	

The UK has an extensive range of national newspapers as well as a number of daily **regional newspapers**. Modern technology enables newspapers to be produced during the night and front page stories can be changed quickly as events emerge. This helps to explain the importance and impact of our newspapers on people's understanding of events. If you study a range of national daily newspapers it is easy to see that they appeal to different audiences according to their news stories and through their use of language, photographs and headlines. A number of national newspapers support different major political parties and this is illustrated in the way that they report political stories. Traditionally, the **quality newspapers** have helped to set the national political agenda, but increasingly politicans of all parties wish to receive positive press coverage in the **popular press**.

 Why is it more important for politicians to get coverage in *The Sun* rather than *The Guardian*?

GLOSSARY

Popular press: Sometimes referred to as the tabloid press, due to the actual size of the newspaper. Mass circulation newspapers that contain a range of different types of news, sport and popular news stories. Their cover price is normally less than that of the quality press.

Quality press: Name given to the traditional broadsheet newspapers, due to their fuller size. They contain a larger range of news stories from the UK and abroad and cover news relating to the business world. They are more expensive than the popular papers and contain more pages.

Regional press: Newspapers that appear either daily, in the evenings or weekly, and are printed in different parts of the UK. They contain a range of national and regional news stories.

Questions

1. Do you think that the *News of the World* was right to 'name and shame'?
2. How do you think newspapers influence the way people vote?
3. Why do newspapers report the same event in different ways?
4. How do popular national daily newspapers differ from the quality national daily newspapers?

Have I Got News for You?

Protection from the Media

KEY ISSUES

- Do citizens have a right to privacy?
- Should the power of the press be curbed?

Curbing the Freedom of the Press

The popular press in the UK likes to publish stories about the rich and famous. In Britain the press is left to regulate itself through the **Press Complaints Commission** (PCC). This is an independent body made up of representatives from the newspaper industry, public representatives and an independent chair. It was set up in the early 1990s after the government threatened to introduce legislation to control the press after public concern about a number of popular press newspaper stories.

What Would Your Verdict Have Been?

1 *The Daily Telegraph* revealed that the Prime Minister's son, Euan Blair, was interviewed for a place at Oxford University College. The Blairs complained.

The Telegraph's defence was that of **public interest**, especially because Oxford University's admission policy had been criticised by the occupant of No. 11 Downing Street – the Chancellor of the Exchequer, Gordon Brown. The PCC upheld the complaint saying that the article was an unnecessary intrusion.

2 The *Sunday People* published a set of nude photos of Sara Cox, a radio presenter, and her husband on honeymoon. The paper's editor apologised. Sara Cox decided that was not sufficient and took legal action.

The *Daily Star*, which published semi-nude pictures of the actress Amanda Holden, paid out £40,000 in damages and £75,000 in costs in a recent out-of-court settlement.

INFO BOX

RIGHT TO PRIVACY

In 1978, Gordon Kaye the actor, was photographed in hospital suffering from serious head injuries. His claim against the *Sunday Sport* was dismissed in 1990. The court ruled that 'there was no right to privacy'.

Judges now have to interpret the 'Right to Privacy' as defined in the Human Rights Act 1998.

3 Naomi Campbell, a famous model, took the *Daily Mirror* to court over their publication of a photograph, which showed her leaving a meeting of Narcotics Anonymous. The case was brought on grounds of privacy and breach of confidence. While she won her case and a small amount of damages, the trial also resulted in a lot of negative publicity about Campbell's life, which was published in the newspapers. On appeal, the original verdict was overturned.

▲ The right to privacy – Naomi Campbell.

▲ Sara Cox, DJ.

Privacy 2002?

A national pop star competition 'Pop Idol', attracted millions of viewers over several weeks and more young people voted to decide the winner of the competition than voted in the 2001 General Election. Within

▲ Will Young.

weeks of winning, Will Young announced that he is gay. Young, whose first record became the fastest-selling debut single in UK history, told reporters that 'media pressure' led him to talk about his private life: 'I don't wish to talk about it any further … my private life is my private life'.

Does the Government Need to Act?

Unless the government defines the privacy situation through legislation, the law will be constructed from piecemeal decisions by the courts. The court's decision to protect the new identities of the killers of James Bulger was criticised in the press (see p. 64).

The Case of Mary Bell

Thirty years ago Mary Bell, at the age of 11, was imprisoned for the murder of a 3-year-old boy. She suffered years of abuse and appalling treatment in England's prisons. After her release at the age of 23, she lived in fear of her new identity being revealed. In 1998, *The Times* serialised a book about the Mary Bell case by the author Gitta Sereny. Some newspapers, due to the interest in child killers, decided to find out Mary's whereabouts and to print the story. *The Sun* found where Mary lived and the press gathered outside her home. Mary's 14-year-old daughter then discovered about her mother's past. Within hours the family was forced into hiding.

In the James Bulger case was the judge right? In the Mary Bell case was the press right to pursue her and her family?

INFO BOX

COMPLAINING ABOUT THE PRESS

The Press Council deals with complaints about what is published in UK newspapers.

The Press Complaints Commission can only decide on issues that contravene its Code Of Conduct. Some of its main points are:

- Accuracy. The press have a duty to print accurate reports.
- Opportunity to reply. People should be given a fair opportunity to reply, if reasonable.
- Privacy. No intrusion into people's private lives.
- Payments for articles. No witness or potential witness should be paid.
- Harassment. The press must not intimidate or harass.
- Children under 16 should not be interviewed or photographed without the permission of their parents.
- Children in sex cases. Victims under 16 must not be identified, even if the law allows it.
- Victims of crime should not be identified unless the law permits it.
- Discrimination. Reference to all types of discrimination should be avoided.
- Confidential sources should be protected.

Newspapers are allowed to claim that a story is in the 'public interest', even when in some cases it seems to contravene the Code.

GLOSSARY

Press Complaints Commission: Independent watchdog of the press industry, established and run by the industry.

Public Interest: The right of the press to publish stories because the newspaper claims that the stories are of public interest.

Questions

1 Is it right for the newspaper industry to regulate itself through the Press Complaints Commission?
2 Do famous people and their families have a right to privacy?
3 How would you decide what is in the 'public interest', when deciding what a newspaper could print?

The Power of Television

KEY ISSUES

○ How powerful and influential is television?
○ What is the impact of TV on our lives?

If You Want the Truth, Turn on the TV?

By law and charter, the **terrestrial TV** channels in the UK have a duty to be politically neutral. Most people trust television news to be fair and unbiased. Due to this and the nature of TV, its universal coverage and the amount of time we spend watching it, it can influence our views and perceptions.

Many would argue that television's power to influence is greater than that of the press, because of its immediacy and its ability to use both images and sound.

Television can be a positive force for good:

• Some years, ago a BBC play called 'Cathy Come Home' was broadcast. It showed the problems of homelessness. Partly as a result, a pressure group called 'Shelter' was formed to campaign about housing issues. Shelter is still campaigning today.

• Following a campaign by Esther Rantzen regarding children and young people in trouble or danger, a new organisation call 'ChildLine' was founded.

ChildLine

0800 1111

◀ ChildLine helps young people in trouble or danger.

ℹ INFO BOX

NUMBER OF HOURS OF TELEVISION VIEWING

Average Weekly Viewing per Person	
BBC1	6hr 29min
BBC2	2hr 29min
ITV	6hr 54min
Ch4	2hr 33min
Ch5	1hr 15min
Other	3hr 33min
TOTAL	**23hr 15min**

Source: BRAD (British Rate and Data), October 1999.

▲ South Park.

▲ Eastenders.

▲ ITN newscasters Dermot Murnaghan and Kirsty Young.

▲ Darren Campbell wins Gold.

- In 1984, Michael Buerke, a BBC News Correspondent, did a special report on a famine in Ethiopia. This was instrumental in the organisation of the international Live Aid Concerts, which raised over £60 million.

▲ Live Aid Concert.

- Both BBC and ITV help to raise millions of pounds for charities through the Children in Need Appeal and Red Nose Day.

INFO BOX

ARE WE WHAT WE WATCH?

Top viewing figures	
BBC1 Casualty	7.93 million
BBC2 Gardeners World	3.50 million
ITV Heartbeat	10.27 million
The soaps	
Coronation Street	12.86 million
EastEnders	11.90 million
Emmerdale Farm	9.20 million
Satellite	
Cup Special	1.24 million

Source BARB (Broadcasters Audience Research Board Ltd.), April 2002.

What the News Tells Us!

Most viewers rely upon the television to find out about news from around the world. However, to what extent do the stories that appear on television help us to understand the background of the news story?

The story of the Arab/Israeli dispute was analysed by the Glasgow University Media Group, to find out how the events in Israel and Palestine, as reported on television, were understood by a sample of 300 young people. The results indicated that a lack of explanation about the origins of the conflict, and the different use of language often to describe the same events, affected people's understanding; as one young person stated:

'You always think of the Palestinians as being really aggressive because of the stories you hear on the news. I always put the blame on them in my own head'.

INFO BOX

THE NEW MEDIA
This is a term that is now used to describe all forms of electronic technologies, ranging from traditional ones like television, radio and telephone which are becoming digital to the newer forms such as the internet, interactive television, CD-ROM and streaming audio.

GLOSSARY

Terrestrial television: Television from a UK-land based organisation, i.e. BBC, ITV, Channels 4 and 5.

Satellite television: Television via a satellite dish from a commercial company, i.e. Sky TV.

Questions

1. How does television influence the way we behave and respond to situations?
2. Which is the more powerful influence – TV or the press?
3. Do we watch too much television? Does it influence too much of our thinking?
4. What impact do you think the new media will have on our lives?

Pressure for Change

Local Protest

KEY ISSUES

○ Can you make a difference locally?
○ How do pressure groups attract public attention?
○ How should the government react to pressure group ideas and tactics?

This Green and Pleasant Land

'NIMBY' is a word often used to describe people who do not want any changes in their local area. Often they are not opposed to the change, but they think it should take place elsewhere. NIMBY means 'Not In My Back Yard'. Every local council regularly has to draw up plans for new housing and industrial developments. Even if the local councils do not want any changes, if the government has decided that new developments are required, local councils must decide where they go and produce, after public consultation, a Development Plan for their area.

Devon County Council was told by the government that Devon needed to build 99,000 new homes between 1991 and 2011. The county council and the district councils in Devon said that the figure was far too high and, after much pressure, the figure was reduced to 91,800. The council then had to decide how to spread out these new houses between the cities, towns and villages of Devon, or whether the county should construct new communities.

The county council decided to opt for **new towns**, one of which was to be built in the South Hams, near the major city of Plymouth. Immediately, those living near the proposed new town site formed a protest group, SHARD (South Hams Against Rural Destruction). From its first public meeting, SHARD campaigned in a variety of ways to fight the proposed developments.

What Elements Make Up a Successful Campaign?

- **Membership** – SHARD, like many other groups, tries to build up a large membership and supporter base. This way it has gained a source of fund-raising, as well as a means of communication.
- **A clear strategy plan** – SHARD contacted local councils and gathered information about the basis of any decisions. By becoming experts about development planning, SHARD were better able to challenge local councils and councillors.
- **Use of the media** – in order to make the general public aware of their concerns, the group issued numerous press releases, spoke on local radio and appeared on regional television. The group held numerous marches and protests, all of which have gained publicity.

▼ Rural South Hams.

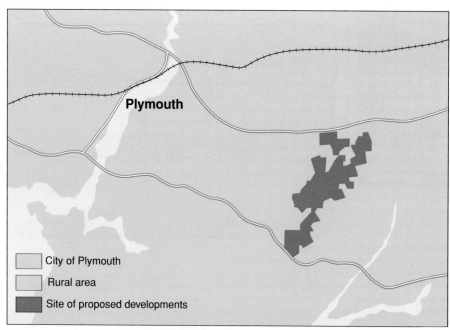

City of Plymouth
Rural area
Site of proposed developments

▼ SHARD protest.

SHARD are still campaigning and provide an example of how ordinary citizens can work on an individual basis or in a group to bring about a change in policy.

GLOSSARY

Pressure group: A group of people who share a common aim and work together to bring about change or prevent change. Pressure groups operate at all levels of our society; local, regional, national and international.

NIMBY: Stands for Not In My Back Yard; a criticism often levelled at local groups who oppose change in their own area.

New towns: A entire new housing or community development, normally built on a greenfield site.

? Questions

1 Why are some local pressure groups more successful than others?
2 i) What other tactics do you think SHARD should adopt?
  ii) Do you agree with SHARD's campaign? Issues to think about include lack of houses for people in the local area, and the impact that the housing will have on the environment and other local communities – will local people be able to afford these houses?
3 Why is media coverage important to any local pressure group?

Pressure for Change

KEY ISSUES

○ Can you make a difference nationally?
○ How do national pressure groups bring about change?
○ How should government react to national protests?

National Protest

As well as trying to stop things happening, protests can bring about change. In recent years political parties have seen a decline in membership, while single-interest protest groups and pressure groups have seen a great increase in interest and membership. The Royal Society for the Protection of Birds (RSPB) has more members than the three major UK political parties.

How Do We Know About Pressure Groups?

As citizens we often only find out about a pressure group when it is reported in the media.

INFO BOX

The horror of the Dunblane killings in Scotland, when a teacher and many of her class were killed by a lone gunman, led to the Snowdrop Campaign, which was supported by the press. A national petition was organised and new **legislation** passed by parliament regarding handgun use and ownership. The legislation also tightened the regulations of gun clubs.

Greenpeace, the international environmental protection group, used to take **direct action** by sailing its ships amongst whaling fleets and providing film footage for the media. It has also built up a excellent reputation for scientific research, and it actively lobbies governments and international organisations to bring about change.

The Downfall of a Prime Minister

In the late 1980s, first people in Scotland and then in England became angry about the new Community Charge (**Poll Tax**) that was being introduced by the Conservative government. This became the major political issue of the day and numerous protest marches were organised by a variety of groups throughout the UK. Some protests got out of hand

and became very violent. MP's post bags were full as people complained about the new tax. However, the Prime Minister, Mrs Thatcher, refused to budge, believing that the new tax was better than its predecessor. The Conservatives were doing badly in the opinion polls and they lost a parliamentary by-election, called the 'Poll Tax By-Election', (see pp. 50–51). In 1990, Mrs Thatcher was challenged for the leadership of the Conservative Party. She withdrew from the race after winning the first ballot, but failing to get enough votes to win outright. John Major won the election and became the leader of the Conservative Party and Prime Minister. One of his first decisions was to reform and rename the Community Charge. It is now called the Council Tax and is still how councils collect local taxes for the services they provide.

Animals have Rights

Alongside environmental issues, the animal rights issue has developed in intensity in recent years. Since 1824, organisations like the Royal Society for the Prevention of Cruelty to Animals (RSPCA) have cared for and campaigned on animal welfare issues. A respected organisation, the RSPCA's views are often canvassed by government. Increasingly the public have become concerned about animal rights, whether hunting with hounds, whaling, over-fishing, factory farms, animal experimentation or the movement of live animals.

In the late 1990s, protests were organised against the export of live animals from UK ports. The media

▲ Massive demonstrations throughout the UK against the export of live animals.

followed the story, and a number of blockades took place at docks and ferry ports. The protests were so successful that many docks ground to a halt and shipping companies refused to accept lorries carrying animals. People of all ages and backgrounds took part in the protests, many protesting in this way for the first time.

A Protest too Far?

Some forms of protest, particularly those involving direct action, are clearly intended to be threatening and are illegal.

In August 1998, 6000 mink were set free from a fur farm by animal liberation activists, to stop them being killed to make fur coats. Mink are vicious predators and households in the area were warned to look after their pets and livestock. The group likened their action to the struggle to abolish slavery and women getting the vote.

 Do you think the animal liberation protesters were justified in their actions?
Discuss why you agree or disagree with others in your class.

The Global Protest

While some organised pressure groups operate on a global scale, for example Greenpeace, global protest appears to be more a product of the 'new media' age. The internet, e-mail and phone texting provide quick and cheap ways for people to pass on information and to organize themselves.

▲ Macdonalds, London on May Day 2000.

Instead of major gatherings of world leaders receiving media coverage of their discussions and decisions, in recent years the coverage has been about the scale of expected 'anti-capitalist' riots and the 'nature of the fortress' the leaders have to meet in. Increasingly international meetings are held in isolated, secure locations. When they are held in city centres, the police have difficulties securing the perimeter around the meeting. The anti-capitalist rioters use May Day, the International Day of the Worker, to hold protests.

INFO BOX

MAY RIOTS – LONDON 2000
- Ninety-seven arrested.
- Cenotaph and statue of Churchill vandalised.
- Nine police hurt.
- 'Criminality and thuggery masquerading as political protest' – Government
- 'Their intention is to disrupt everyday workings of London life' – Sir John Stevens, Metropolitan Police Commissioner.

GLOSSARY

Legislation: A new Act of Parliament – a law.

Poll Tax: Nickname for the Community Charge, a replacement for the domestic rating system and a major source of local government funding.

Direct Action: Action taken by individuals and groups to further their aims. While some tactics like marches and lobbying are lawful, some forms of direct action comprise illegal acts, for example, break-in, use of violence and intimidation.

Questions

1 Why do young people prefer to join single-issue pressure groups, rather than political parties?
2 Is illegal protest ever justified? Use examples in your answer.
3 What are the problems associated with large-scale protests? How do you think the government and the police should react?
4 Do protest groups influence government too much? Give reasons for your answer.

Our Role in the Wider World

KEY ISSUES

○ The EU and the UK – the continuing debate
○ The future of the EU.

The European Ideal?

Following the end of the Second World War politicians across Europe realised that by working together the nation states of Europe might be able to prevent another European war. Europe was already divided by the 'Iron Curtain' which separated the countries of Eastern Europe, under Russian control, from those in the West. Germany was divided into four zones, occupied by the American, French, British and the Russians, with its capital, Berlin, in the middle of the Russian zone, further divided into four zones. Eventually, it became a country of two halves, democratic West Germany and communist East Germany, before finally re-unifying in 1990.

As the countries of Western Europe recovered economically after the war they began to cooperate to develop their industries more efficiently. In 1957 the Treaty of Rome established a European Community of six members: France, Germany, Italy, Belgium, Holland and Luxembourg. Its aims were to seek economic expansion and create a common internal market for one another's goods.

Initially the UK remained outside the European Community. In the 1960s its application for membership was twice rejected by the French on the grounds that 'we weren't European enough, more concerned with our relationship across the Atlantic', meaning the USA who has traditionally been our close ally. The UK became a member in 1973 and the first national referendum was held in 1975 on our continuing membership which was supported with a 2:1 majority.

In 2002 the European Union (**EU**) had 15 members and a further 12 from Central and Eastern Europe had applied and begun preparations for entry. Turkey was also accepted as an applicant, but had not begun membership negotiations. (For more information on the EU see p. 45.)

▲ The European Union.

Who Gets What?

One of the functions of the EU is to give assistance to the poorer areas of the EU. Over a third of its budget goes on this work across Europe and parts of the UK, e.g. Cornwall, Wales and Scotland benefit from this aid. The largest consumer of EU funds is the Agricultural budget. Only 5 per cent of the EU workforce is employed in agriculture but it receives 44.5 per cent of the EU budget. The UK receives 9.9 per cent compared to France's 23.8 per cent of the Agricultural budget of 41.5bn Euros.

Europe produces more than it can consume and it is recognised that there is an urgent need to reform the Common Agricultural Policy (**CAP**) especially as some of the new entrants, such as Poland, have large agricultural sectors.

Why Do People Get So Angry About The EU?

* Some people believe the EU, based in Brussels, is taking away the power of our national government to decide things in the UK.
* The growth of the single internal market has led some countries to call for a common taxation system across Europe. This would mean that individual countries would have, for example, the same levels of income tax, VAT and other excise duties. This would offer a fairer trading market, but leave less power for individual governments.
* The development of a single European currency (the Euro) means that individual countries have less independence regarding their own economic policy, i.e.

what they can spend or borrow as a country. If the Euro was used by all countries in the EU it would become, with the Dollar, one of the two major world currencies. It would enable fairer trade within the EU, and a common interest rate for all, because all business would be competing on a more level playing field regarding costs outside their control. The disadvantages are that it takes away power over economic policy for national politicians and governments.

- Some people believe that Europe and its decision-makers are remote from the electorate and out of touch with the feelings of ordinary people, hence the low turnout in European Parliamentary elections.
- Others believe that the EU is undemocratic, that it is controlled by the industrial states, not the Members of European Parliament (MEPs).

The other side of the coin

- Whenever countries join international organisations they agree to pool some national interests e.g. World Trade Organisation, for the benefit of the world economic system.
- The single market enables businesses and individuals to compete on a level playing field. If taxes were the same the most efficient businesses would gain trade, because businesses would be competing only on the price and quality of their goods, as taxes and interest and currency rates would be the same for all.

- If you have a single market, with a single interest rate system, a single currency makes sense. Businesses and individuals can compete more equally. Imagine if every state of the USA had a different currency!

The Future of the European Union

The most important question facing Europe is whether the countries of Europe work more closely together and share more power with the EU. In other words we work towards a United States of Europe (a **Federal** structure) or by allowing more countries to join the Union become less centralised and more informal.

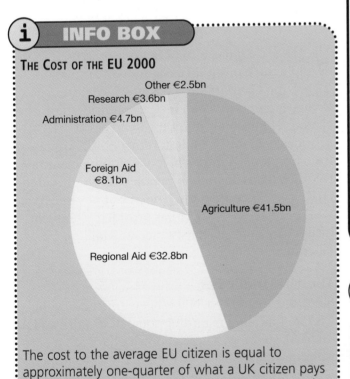

INFO BOX

THE COST OF THE EU 2000

- Other €2.5bn
- Research €3.6bn
- Administration €4.7bn
- Foreign Aid €8.1bn
- Agriculture €41.5bn
- Regional Aid €32.8bn

The cost to the average EU citizen is equal to approximately one-quarter of what a UK citizen pays in Council Tax a year to run their local councils and police.

GLOSSARY

CAP: Common Agricultural Policy of the EU. Largest spending area of the EU. Very controversial especially in the UK. Provides financial support for farmers.

EU: The European Union – superseded the EEC (European Economic Community – known as the Common Market). Currently comprises 15 members, and aims to encourage trade and provide a common internal market.

European Commission: Made up of Commissioners appointed by member states. The UK has two, who work under the President of the Commission, appointed by the member states to run the bureaucracy of the EU and help determine policy.

European Parliament: Directly elected by the voters of the EU. Sit in trans-national party group, i.e. Labour with the Socialist Group, the Conservatives in the Christian Democrat Group, the Liberal Democrat in the Liberal and Radical Group. The parliament has limited powers.

Federalism: A formal political structure where power is shared between central and local government, e.g. USA and Germany. Used in the UK to donate more power to the EU and less to the UK government.

Questions

1. Why do so many people oppose the idea of a United States of Europe?
2. How do you think citizens can have more influence within the EU?
3. What are the advantages and the disadvantages of the UK belonging to the EU?

KEY ISSUES

○ The EU and the UK – the continuing debate
○ The UK on the world stage as a member of the UN

A New World Order

Twice in the twentieth century World War has broken out because of disputes between the nations of Europe. Tens of millions of members of the armed forces and civilians have died. By the end of the Second World War a new world order was emerging, where *two* super-powers would dominate the world stage, the USA and the **USSR** (now known as Russia and the former Soviet States).

Those countries we know as the 'Allies' during the Second World War (Britain, France, the US and USSR) also used the name 'the United Nations' (**UN**). The term described the organisation that assembled on 24 October 1945 in New York after the end of the Second World War. One of the UN's central functions was to persuade countries to resolve their differences without resorting to violence. If need be, the UN could raise armed forces from its member countries to fight aggression.

The UN, as well as attempting to preserve the peace, was expected to establish a framework that would lead to the 'economic and social advancement of all peoples'. When it was established, the UN had two key deliberative bodies: the **General Assembly** to which all members sent representatives and the **Security Council** which was made up of five permanent members and a larger number elected from the assembly of other countries on a regular basis. The five permanent members are the USA, Russia, China, France and the UK. These five members also have the power to 'veto' any decision of the Council.

The Work of the UN

As well as direct armed involvement aimed at resolving conflicts (like that which occurred in Korea) the UN often provide 'peacekeeping' forces throughout the world to act as a buffer between armies of opposing countries or factions within countries in the case of civil wars. This happens

▲ The UN also distributes food during times of war or famine.

when agreements have been reached between opposing sides, such as between the Greek and Turkish forces in Cyprus, or Serbian and Croat armies in the former Yugoslavia. These forces often come from countries that are otherwise neutral, for example the Republic of Ireland. The work of the UN affects many spheres of everyday life. Much of its work is carried out by specialist agencies.

The UN set standards for a better world, for example the Universal Declaration of Human Rights, the Conventions on Women, Children, Refugees and Genocide. In 122 countries the United Nations High Commission for Refugees (UNHCR) provides help for 22 million refugees. UN volunteers from over 130 countries help developing countries. UNAIDS helps 33 million people suffering from the HIV virus. Since 1950 the United Nations Relief and Works Agency (UNRWA) has provided schooling, health care and relief assistance to 3 million Palestinian refugees.

The UN Under Fire

Since the 1980s the UN has been criticised by the USA and its allies regarding some of its work and its internal workings. These countries have often withdrawn financial contributions and favoured non-UN bodies to work with where they have greater influence, such as the World Bank, World Trade Organisation and the International Monetary Fund.

▲ Blue Helmets UN Forces in action.

▲ UN HQ in New York.

The UN budget is less than the New York Fire and Police Service combined and is currently owed 2.5 billion dollars by its member states. Over half of this money is owed by the USA.

ℹ️ INFO BOX

THE UN's ACHIEVEMENTS
1 Maintaining peace and security. Has deployed over 40 peace keeping forces
2 Negotiating 172 peaceful settlements of disputes
3 Promoting Democracy. Helped set up free and fair elections in 45 countries
4 UN Development Programme (UNDP) supports 5000 projects
5 Promoting Human Rights, Universal Declaration of Human rights 1948
6 Protecting the environment e.g. Earth Summit at Rio de Janeiro in 1992
7 Preventing nuclear proliferation. Representatives of the UN inspect nuclear reactors in 90 countries
8 Promoting self determination and independence in many countries that are now member states
9 Strengthening international law. It has aided over 300 agreements and treaties
10 Handing down judicial decisions through the work of the International Court of Justice

GLOSSARY

General Assembly of the UN: An assembly of representatives of all the member states. Meets annually. Resolutions made by them are not binding to members.

Security Council: Main UN peace keeping body made up of five permanent members – UK, USA, Russia, France and China – with ten others elected every two years by the Assembly.

UN: United Nations Organisation – based in New York. A forum for the countries of the world. Carries out a peace keeping and humanitarian role.

USSR: Union of Soviet Socialist Republics, of which the largest part was Russia. Name used when under Communist control.

❓ Questions

1 What is the case for the UK still having 'veto' powers at the UN?
2 In what ways has the UN helped preserve the peace since 1945?
3 Has the UN made a difference? If so, why are many of the world's population hungry and poor?
4 What powers do you think the UN should have over national governments?

The Extended British Family?

KEY ISSUES

○ What is the importance of the British Commonwealth?
○ How does the Commonwealth exert international pressure to bring about change?

The Commonwealth

The present-day Commonwealth considers itself a unique 'family' of 54 nations, including both developed and developing countries. Its members' population (1.7 billion) make up 30 per cent of the world's population and it comprises states from all over the world, of many races, languages and cultures. The Queen is Head of State in Britain and 15 other member countries. Its headquarters is at the Commonwealth Secretariat in London, but its meetings are held throughout the world. Over 50 per cent of Britain's direct foreign aid goes to Commonwealth countries.

The aims of the Commonwealth are to advance democracy, human rights and sustainable economic and social development in its member countries. The Commonwealth has no constitution or charter, but the heads of government of the member states meet every two years to discuss issues of common interest. Every four years the Commonwealth Games are held, a major international athletics event. The Commonwealth is a *voluntary* association of independent states. South Africa rejoined in 1994, after an absence of 33 years, and Mozambique has joined, even though it was a former Portuguese colony.

It has been criticised for having little influence and no ability to change the policies of government of member states. The Commonwealth doesn't act as an international bloc vote – they don't vote together as one bloc in international bodies – and has little influence over non-members, but within the Commonwealth, the benefits of membership enable it to exert influence over member countries:

- It campaigned against **apartheid** in South Africa.
- In 1993 it suspended Nigeria after the military regime sentenced writers who were critical of the government to death.

- In 2000 it suspended Fiji following overthrow of the elected government.
- In 2002 it suspended Zimbabwe after the country's presidential elections were seen to be unfair.

Membership also brings practical benefits through the Commonwealth Fund for Technical Co-operation (CFTC) which helps to alleviate poverty.

A Black and White Issue – Bringing South Africa in from the Cold

South Africa was a part of the British Empire, having been formed in 1910 from the Cape Colony, Natal, Transvaal and the Orange Free State, a merger of states either controlled by people from a British or Dutch (Boer) background. In 1912 what was to become the ANC (African National Congress) was formed to promote the rights of the black majority of South Africans.

In 1948 The Afrikaner National Party won the General Election and introduced apartheid policies. These were laws based upon the belief that the races in South Africa should be separated and treated differently. In 1952 the ANC started a campaign of passive peaceful resistance to apartheid. In 1960 African and coloured representation in the parliament of South Africa was banned. Black and coloured people could only live in certain areas. The school you went to was based upon your race. Non-whites were not allowed in certain shops or restaurants; even park benches were for whites or non-whites. Every person had to carry an identity card.

In 1961 South Africa left the Commonwealth and became a Republic. In 1964 Nelson Mandela and other ANC leaders were sentenced to life imprisonment for encouraging acts of terrorism against the apartheid regime. In 1976 over 575 people died in Soweto in clashes with police.

ℹ️ INFO BOX

Three elements of the state's apartheid system were:
- The Race Classification Act. Everyone was classified according to their race
- The Mixed Marriages Act. People from different races were not allowed to marry
- The Group Areas Act. Certain races could only live in designated areas.

Internationally there was condemnation of South Africa and many countries officially boycotted the country by ceasing to trade with them. The UK was divided between those who felt they could persuade South Africa to change and those who wanted direct action. Many people boycotted South African goods, and South Africans of all races came to live in England and help lead the protest movement. The Anti-Apartheid movement blocked South African white-only sports teams visiting the UK. One of the leaders of this campaign was Peter Hain, a South African who led the Young Liberal movement. He later joined the Labour Party and is now an MP and member of the Cabinet.

i INFO BOX

BLACK OR WHITE

'They resemble us but in appearance are the colour of pumpkin-porridge …

They are rude of manners and without any graces or refinement …

They carry long sticks of fire. With this they kill and loot from many nations.'

(Zulu impression of first meeting white men in the nineteenth century)

Turned Away from the House of God
One black South African's experience

'The Presbyterian Church in Orange Grove refused me admittance. The policy did not allow Non-whites into the hall. They also said something about the laws of the country.

At the Kensington DRC (Dutch Reform Church), an aged church official bellowed in Afrikaans, 'What soek jy?' (What do you want?) 'I've come to church,' I said. He shoved me violently, shouting for me to get away. I walked off dejected.

A few doors away was the Baptist Church, and as I walked towards it I began to think that people didn't want me to share their church. As I walked in I was tense, waiting for that tap on the shoulder … but instead I was given a hymn book and welcomed into the church. I sat through the service … This up and down treatment wasn't doing my nerves much good.'

(adapted from an anthology of works of Can Themba, entitled *The Will to Die*)

From 1976 to 1977 over 575 people died in confrontations between Africans and the police in Soweto and other African townships. As the international isolation increased internal pressure for change mounted as one by one the former European colonies surrounding South Africa gained independence and were being governed by the native African majority. A new white President, De Klerk, realised that time had run out on the old-style South Africa and started negotiations with the leaders representing all groups in South Africa to bring about a peaceful transfer to majority rule.

In 1990 Nelson Mandela and others were released from prison after 26 years. In 1994 the first non-racial elections were held and the ANC won. On 10 May 1994 Nelson Mandela was sworn in as President of South Africa and formed a government of National Unity, comprising the African majority and white minority parties. As a result of this, De Klerk and Nelson Mandela received the Nobel Peace Prize in 1993.

◄ Nelson Mandela celebrates victory.

GLOSSARY

Apartheid: System of laws based upon the idea of racial separation. Introduced in South Africa in 1947.

Commonwealth: A voluntary association of 54 nations representing 1.7 billion people. All members except one from the former British Empire. Established in 1937.

? Questions

1 Is there still a role and function for the Commonwealth?
2 What is the case for the Commonwealth in future electing its own 'Head of Commonwealth'?
3 Could the Commonwealth and others have done more to end apartheid in South Africa earlier?
4 What arguments can be used *against* the apartheid laws introduced in South Africa?

KEY ISSUES

○ How do individuals get involved in disputes?
○ Why do conflicts occur?
○ How can we resolve conflicts?

Why do we get involved in disputes?

TRUANCY MOTHER JAILED

In May 2002 Patricia Amos, a mother of five, was sentenced in Oxfordshire to serve a prison sentence because she had failed to ensure that two of her daughters attended their secondary school.

After an appeal the sentence passed on Mrs Amos was reduced to 28 days. The children are now attending school. The Local Education Authority had said that they had tried numerous ways of helping Mrs Amos, but she had failed to attend meetings and had broken a parenting order imposed by the court requiring her to make the girls attend school.

The government has made tackling truancy a high priority, and the powers of Magistrates' Courts were increased in November 2000 to impose fines up to £2500.

Was this a successful way to resolve this dispute? How does this case involve issues like rights, responsibilities, power and authority?

Who did this dispute involve?
• Parent
• Government
• School
• Local Education Authority
• Children
• Courts

Sharing

The issues of sharing are a regular source of conflict. Usually this conflict does not go beyond argument and the use of the law. Sometimes, however, the conflict **escalates** and turns into fighting and full-scale war. In the past it is possible to see that some conflict was due to a struggle for sheer survival, for example if there was not enough food to go round. More usually conflicts have arisen for other reasons.

A frequent cause of conflict in a group is when more than one person strives to become *leader*. To avoid this, groups developed rules for selecting leaders.

Another frequent source of conflict is disagreement over how much *power* leaders should have. Today we try to regulate this conflict through political debate and elections. Nevertheless, if some people think things are becoming unfair or that they are not being listened to they may set up pressure groups, wage campaigns or take direct action. Some groups seek to **dominate** other groups. This is a major source of conflict. Civil and international wars have occurred over the years for this reason.

Is conflict always undesirable?

Conflict can be constructive. When people argue about whether more nuclear power stations should be built, or whether euthanasia should be legalised, these arguments can help clarify thinking. If debate is stifled by dictatorship then disagreements gradually build into destructive conflict. Democracy is a major development in managing conflict. Disagreements can be expressed, discussed and voted on.

What are the characteristics of conflicts?

The more people understand that conflicts have certain common characteristics, the more chance there is of finding ways to resolve them: What are these characteristics?

Most disputes go through stages.

The first stage is that the parties to a conflict want something that is mutually exclusive. In other words A believes (s)he can only be satisfied at B's expense and vice-versa. *Next,* a dispute can often escalate into conflict because one or both parties do not actively seek to resolve it. The longer the dispute goes on, the more difficult it becomes to achieve this basic starting point.

If the dispute escalates, one side might be physically stronger than the other and seek to impose a solution that favours one side. This is not the same as resolving the conflict. It may have advantages in the short term. However, it will usually be temporary.

Consider this situation:

Two brothers aged 11 and 13 want to go out skateboarding until 10.30 p.m.
    Their parents say they must do their homework first, and 10.30 p.m. is far too late. The boys think their parents are being unfair.

 How could this dispute escalate or be resolved?

▲ How could this dispute be resolved?

Consequences

Resentment. If one side feels it is being treated unfairly then that is often enough to build up determination not to 'give in'. This may lead to retaliation and the conflict becoming physical, causing people to be hurt and property damaged. Conflicts can have a range of effects, for example people can become depressed, isolated, aggressive and so on.

Once a conflict has developed out of a disagreement then loss of face can become an issue. This means that neither side wants to appear as the loser. This can become a real obstacle when attempting to bring sides together, especially if many people have been affected by the conflict.

How can conflicts be resolved?

Some conflicts which arise out of discrimination or persecution due to prejudice cannot be resolved by **compromise** and require the most resolute resistance combined with patient education and reasoning.

Many conflicts, however, may be resolved when the parties are prepared to negotiate to some degree. The following approaches may help:
- Intermediaries. When parties do not trust each other, other people can be used as intermediaries to get messages across without face-to-face meetings.
- An arbitrator. Someone trusted by both sides who will hear both arguments and come up with a compromise proposal that both sides agree to accept.

Conflict resolution requires parties to recognise that only by compromising can a way forward be found.

GLOSSARY

Compromise: Where the parties to a disagreement set aside elements of their arguments so that an agreement may be reached.

Domination: When an individual, a group, community or nation attempts to exercise power over others, without their agreement.

Escalation: A build-up in misunderstanding and tension between differing groups, which is often linked to the makers of threats and counterthreats.

? Questions

1 Why do disagreements escalate?
2 How do you think it is best to deal with issues where there are differences of opinion between teenagers and their parents?
3 Some people say 'compromising is a sign of weakness'. How would you counter that point of view?
4 Which do you think are the best ways of resolving conflicts?

The UK and Conflict

In recent years the United Kingdom has been involved in several disputes that have involved other nations. Each dispute has been resolved differently, one by direct negotiation, another by the arbitration of others, one by conflict, and one is still to be resolved.

Falklands/Malvinas War

In April 1982, Argentinian armed forces invaded the Falkland Islands in the South Atlantic, a **British dependency**. For over 100 years the Argentinians had laid claim to the Falkland Islands, which they call the Malvinas. In 1982 Argentina was ruled by a military junta, which was becoming increasingly unpopular. The British had only a token force of Royal Marines based in the Falklands and the Argentinians landed thousands of troops. The UK sought United Nations support in condemning the invasion. The Falkland Islands are over 7000 miles from the UK and 3300 miles from the nearest friendly bases in the Ascension Islands.

▲ British troops arriving in the Falkland Islands during the Falklands War.

The UK launched a task force to retake the Falkland Islands. Three nuclear submarines enforced a military exclusion zone until the task force of 65 British ships and 15,000 men arrived.

On 25 April British troops retook South Georgia, one of the outlying islands.

During the ensuing campaign to retake the Islands, the British Navy destroyed over half of the Argentinian combat aircraft and the Argentinian cruiser Belgrano was torpedoed by a British submarine. The British Navy lost several ships as a result of bombing and Exocet missiles.

The conflict ended on 14 June 1982 after a three-week campaign when the Argentines surrendered. Partly as a result of the war the military junta lost power in Argentina.

The British lost 238 lives in the campaign. The Falkland Islanders have always indicated that they wish to remain British citizens and that the islands remain British.

How can the issue be resolved? The UK now maintain a large military presence in the Falklands. In 1993 the UK and Argentina signed an agreement regarding oil and gas exploration in the South-West Atlantic. The Falkland Islands, which had been in decline, now has an increasing population, is becoming a tourist location and is funded by money raised from its sale of fishing rights. In 1998 the Argentinian President visited the UK.

Hong Kong – A Peaceful Hand-over

In 1842 the British took over Hong Kong Island and in 1898 leased other land called the New Territories on a 99-year **lease**.

Since the Second World War Hong Kong has become a thriving economic centre. It is one of the world's largest exporters. In 1984 the UK government and the Communist government of China agreed that **sovereignty** of Hong Kong would revert back to China in 1997. Not only did the UK hand over the New Territories, it handed back Hong Kong. Why did it do this? It was necessary because the infrastructure connecting all the islands meant that Hong Kong

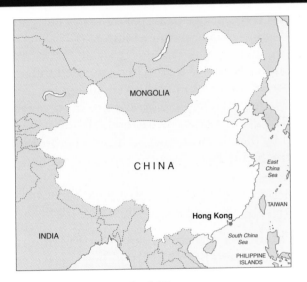

▲ Hong Kong and mainland China.

▲ Gibraltar in relation to Spain.

could not survive on its own. The handover also allowed the British government to negotiate with the Chinese government over the future of the islands.

An agreement was reached whereby the 'life style' of Hong Kong would remain unchanged for 50 years and that the territory would enjoy a high degree of self government, and would not have the communist system or policies imposed upon it.

Gibraltar – 'Between a Rock and a Hard Place'?

Gibraltar was handed over to Britain in the Treaty of Utrecht (1713) following British occupation in 1704. Gibraltar is a 6.5 sq km outcrop from Southern Spain, with a population of 30,000. For many years Spain has claimed sovereignty over Gibraltar and from 1969 to 1985 it closed its frontier gates to Gibraltar. Gibraltar was the British Navy's fortress and gateway into the Mediterranean. It is still an important military base for the British.

Recently the British government commenced talks with the Spanish government about the future of Gibraltar. Any discussions are subject to the agreement of the people of Gibraltar who have clearly stated that they want no change in their status. When they last voted on the issue in 1967, 12,138 voted for no change in their status and 44 against.

As Spain and the United Kingdom are members of the EU, both sides would like to resolve this long-outstanding issue.

 Can they proceed against the wishes of the people of Gibraltar?

GLOSSARY

British Dependency: Parts of the former British Empire that are controlled and run by the UK government.

Lease: An agreement to rent or have use of something for a fixed period of time.

Sovereignty: The right of a country to control its own future and political structure.

? Questions

1 What issues and problems link these three case studies?
2 How and why did the UK react differently to the problem of Hong Kong and the Falkland Islands?
3 Who should decide the future of Gibraltar?
4 How do you think international disputes like these should be resolved?

KEY ISSUES

○ How individuals have made a difference and have a worldwide impact
○ How individuals made a difference in Northern Ireland

People Who Have Made a Difference

Sometimes people gain a worldwide reputation by their actions and approaches to resolving conflict. Three such international individuals are Mohandas Gandhi, Martin Luther King and Nelson Mandela. In 1998 two Northern Ireland politicians, John Hume and David Trimble, won the Nobel Peace Prize for their contribution to conflict resolution.

Mohandas K Gandhi was born in 1869 in India. He came to London and trained as a lawyer. He moved to South Africa and worked hard to improve the rights of immigrant Indian workers. It was at this time that he developed his ideas of **passive resistance**, the use of non-violent action against injustice. He was frequently jailed in South Africa.

In 1915 he took a leading role in the campaign for Indian independence from the British. When Muslim or Hindu supporters committed acts of violence, he would fast until the violence ended. In 1947 the British granted India independence, but fighting broke out between the Hindus and Muslims and the country was partitioned into India and Pakistan. Gandhi continued to fast to stop the rioting. He was assassinated, aged 79, in January 1948, when he was about to take evening prayers. The assassin was an Indian who opposed Gandhi's religious tolerance.

Martin Luther King was a black American who led the main struggle for racial equality that ended segregation in the USA.

In 1957 he founded the Southern Christian Leadership Conference calling for a non-violent struggle against racism. Even though the US Supreme Court ruled against **segregation** in 1954, many aspects of life, especially in the southern states of the USA, continued along segregated lines. Rosa Parks, a black woman, was thrown off a bus and fined for refusing to give up her seat to a white man.

Six-year-old Ruby Bridges was spat on for wanting to go to the same school as white children.

Martin Luther King was a preacher who used the power base of the black church to campaign for change. He led marches and boycotts to bring about change. His life was often threatened. He was hounded by the FBI, who bugged his phone. In 1964 he won the Nobel Peace Prize.

He was assassinated in 1968 in Memphis. Since 1983 his birthday has been a national holiday in the USA.

Nelson Mandela – from Prisoner to President

Nelson Mandela was born in 1918 in the Transkei in South Africa. He trained as a lawyer. In 1944 he joined the anti-apartheid African National Congress (ANC) (see pp. 82–83) and led a campaign of passive resistance against the South African government. In 1962 he was imprisoned by the government. In the dock he said:

'During my lifetime I have dedicated myself to the struggle of the African people. I have fought against white domination, and I have fought against black domination. I have cherished the ideal of a democratic and free society in which all persons live together in harmony and with equal opportunities. It is an ideal I hope to achieve. But, if need be, it is an ideal for which I am prepared to die.'

From 1962 until 1990 he was imprisoned with other leading members of the ANC. Eventually the South African president, F W de Klerk held talks with Nelson Mandela, and he and his fellow prisoners were released.

Together F W de Klerk and Nelson Mandela prepared South Africa for majority black rule. In 1994 Mandela was elected president of South Africa, having shared the Nobel Peace Prize with F W de Klerk in 1993.

▲ Nelson Mandela   ▲ Mohandas Gandhi

Northern Ireland

Ireland was partitioned in 1922 into the Irish Free State (Eire) in the South, and Northern Ireland, often known as Ulster, which remained a part of the UK. Although Northern Ireland had its own parliament, **Nationalists** in both parts of Ireland continued to campaign and fight for a 'united Ireland' independent of the UK.

Following disputes over civil rights in the North in 1968, the UK government sent in British troops to maintain the peace between the Nationalists and the **Unionists** in the North. For nearly 30 years after the civil unrest in 1968 a campaign of violence was waged in Northen Ireland, Eire and the UK mainland by the opposing **terrorist** groups.

In 1985 the Anglo-Irish Agreement was signed by the UK and Irish prime ministers, establishing a framework for future discussions. In 1993 the Anglo-Irish Declaration laid out a framework for a peaceful agreement to the troubles of Northen Ireland, based upon the idea of 'consent', that any agreement can only proceed if it is agreed by the people of Northen Ireland. In 1996 former US Senator George Mitchell agreed to chair the Northen Ireland peace talks. David Trimble, the leader of the Ulster Unionist Party, and John Hume of the Social Democratic and Labour Part (SDLP), a Nationalist Party, put years of mistrust aside to help broker the agreement. After all-party talks an agreement was announced on Good Friday 1998. A new Assembly was created in Northen Ireland, and power was again transferred back from London to Belfast. Referendums in both Northern Ireland and Eire support the agreement.

What factors helped to resolve the troubles in Northern Ireland?

i INFO BOX

CAMPAIGN OF TERROR

1971	February	First solider shot dead in Northen Ireland.
	December	15 people killed in attack on Belfast pub (Ulster Volunteer Force)
1972	January	13 Catholic protesters killed by British troops
	July	9 killed in 22 IRA bombs in Belfast
1974	May	22 killed in car bombs in Dublin
	October	5 killed in a Guildford pub
	November	21 killed in two Birmingham pubs
1978	February	12 killed in a hotel in County Down
1979	March	Tory MP Airey Neave killed in car bomb attack
	August	Lord Mountbatten killed when his boat was blown up 19 people died when a bomb exploded under a bus
1981	May	10 Republican (Nationalist) prisoners starve to death
1984	October	5 killed when IRA bomb Tory Party Conference hotel
1987	November	11 killed during Remembrance service in Enniskillen
1988	March	Three IRA suspects shot by British Special Forces in Gibraltar
1990	July	Ian Gow, Tory MP, murdered by IRA car bomb
1993	March	Warrington – 2 children killed by IRA bomb
1996	February	IRA bomb Canary Wharf, London killing 2 people
	July	Manchester – IRA bomb shopping centre

GLOSSARY

Nationalist: People in Ireland who support a single independent state for the whole of Ireland.

Passive Resistance: A policy of campaigning using non-violent means even if your opponents use violence against you.

Segregation: Discrimination against people on the grounds of their race or colour.

Terrorists: Those who use illegal and violent means to pursue their political agenda.

Unionist: Those people who live in Northern Ireland and support the unity of Northern Ireland with the UK.

◀ Murals painted by supporters of rival groups adorn the walls of many buildings in Northern Ireland.

? Questions

1 What do you think still needs to be done to maintain the peace in Northern Ireland?
2 Why are Gandhi, Luther King and Mandela important world figures?
3 Who could you currently nominate for the Nobel Peace Prize and why?

Israel

KEY ISSUES

○ What causes neighbouring peoples to engage in conflict?
○ Can outsiders help resolve conflict?

▲ The West Bank Jewish settlement of Ofarim.

The proposed Jewish State
The proposed Arab State
Jerusalem and its suburbs: to be an international zone
- - - - The Green Line

LEBANON

SYRIA

Haifa

Lake Tiberius

Nazareth

Mediterranean Sea

Jenin

Nablus

Tel Aviv
Jaffa

WEST BANK

TRANSJORDAN

Ramallah

Jerusalem

Gaza City
GAZA
Khan Younis

Hebron

Dead Sea

Beersheba

● El Arish

ISRAEL

EGYPT

NEGEV

▲ Israel.

He cannot forget that Palestinians have tried to destroy his people so he does not find looking for a fair solution easy. Some of his closest friends in the army have been killed.

Ruth lives in a Jewish settlement in the West Bank. There is a military escort for the bus that takes her to school because outside the settlement there are always groups of hostile Palestinians. She remembers a rock being thrown through their car window on the way to the dentist. She will only refer to Palestinians as Arabs. She believes there is no way of proving who is right in the claim to the disputed land but she thinks the Arabs should leave and go to live in some other Arab country.

Her idea of true peace is where they would not have to be afraid of the Arabs. They would not need a military escort to go to school.

Jacob is an Israeli who lives near Jerusalem. He is a member of Peace Now and has met and talked to Palestinians. As a result he understands better how they feel. At school, though, he is called a traitor and persecuted for being soft on Palestinians. His parents' car was vandalised. So now he is in conflict with other Jews. He thinks the only way forward is if more Palestinians and Jews actually meet each other face to face and talk.

In November 1947 the United Nations voted to partition Palestine into Jewish- and Arab-controlled areas. The Jews accepted the plan but the Palestinians and the surrounding Arab countries rejected it.

A Zionist speaks in 1947

'Only when we are living in our own land ruled by Jews will we be safe. "Israel" is Hebrew for "The promised land". It is written in our most holy of books that we should live here.

Have you any idea what horrors we have been through? Six million of us from all over Europe and Russia wiped out by the Nazis.

We have had to be prepared for resistance from the Arabs especially now they have formed terrorist groups, and betrayal by the British. So, of course we must arm ourselves. Who ever heard of a national state without a proper army?

The Palestinian Arabs have plenty of Arab neighbours they can go and live with. Why do they have to live here? We are very disappointed in the British, they have gone back on the word they gave in 1916.

Well, the main thing is the US are on our side. They will back us.'

i INFO BOX

THE BACKGROUND TO EVENTS FROM THE ISRAELI VIEWPOINT

✿ 1947 – the United Nations proposed that Palestine should be divided to try to resolve the conflict between the Zionists (Israelis) and the Palestinians. The USA strongly supported partition.

✿ 1947 – the State of Israel came into existence. Armies from the surrounding Arab states attacked Israel but were defeated and Palestinian Arabs left Israel. The Israelis called this the War of Independence.

Over the next 20 years the surrounding Arab countries fought wars from time to time on behalf of the Palestinians. Each war was won by the Israelis and each time they captured more land.

Israel felt constantly under threat, and was not afraid to use its military power if it felt threatened. It was greatly helped by the USA which gave it $3 billion of aid each year.

Since the founding of the Palestine Liberation Organisation (**PLO**) in 1964, Israel has endured a large number of acts of terrorism from the PLO and other groups. In 1972 11 Israeli athletes were murdered.

Each act of terrorism against Israel has led to a military response by Israel against Palestinian targets.

✿ 1977 – the Egyptian President flew to Israel and agreed to make peace with Israel. The US President Jimmy Carter brokered talks at Camp David in the USA to help develop the peace process. The Egyptian President was later assassinated in Egypt.

✿ 1993 – an agreement was reached in Oslo which offered guidelines for a peace process that was to be finalised by 1998.

As 1998 approached extremists on both sides felt the agreement required them to give up too much and took steps to derail the peace process. By 2001 violent exchanges became a regular pattern of events, including suicide bombing by the Palestinians and bombing, shelling and occupation of Palestinian areas for periods of time by the Israeli army.

▲ Israeli tanks blocking access into Bethlehem.

GLOSSARY

PLO: Palestine Liberation Organisation – a political movement with a military element that seeks the establishment of a Palestinian state.

Zionist: A supporter of the establishment of a Jewish state.

? Questions

1   How has Israel reacted to attacks on its people and what has been the impact of the Israeli actions?
2   Why is there so much mistrust between the Israelis and Palestinians?
3   Why will the USA be so influential in any resolution of this conflict?
4   What countries other than the USA do you think can influence the outcome of this conflict and why?

The Israelis believe that they have the right to exist and live at peace with their neighbours and be free from terrorist attacks. However, many Israelis also believe that the former borders of Israel should be extended to include what they consider to be more like the natural 'biblical' state of Israel.

Palestine

KEY ISSUES

○ What causes neighbouring peoples to engage in conflict?
○ Can outsiders help resolve conflict?

Maysoon was born in a Palestinian refugee camp in the West Bank and has lived there all her life. There are about 3 million Palestinian refugees of whom about 1 million live in camps in Israel.

'My family originally came from Malha, a village near Jerusalem. They had orchards, olive groves, vineyards and fields. In 1948 the Israeli army took over the village and destroyed most of the houses. They even dug up the cemetery and removed the remains of the ancestors ...'

She describes the attacks on the refugee camp by the Israeli airforce. She says she can never forgive the Israelis for that. She says that the Jews will have to learn to share the land. It will take a long time for the bad feelings between Jews and Palestinians to heal. She longs for the freedom of movement and security that comes with real peace.

Monzir lives in Gaza with his family. He was about eight when the **Intafada** started. He joined other young people throwing stones. He describes how the Israelis imposed curfews to try to keep control. Palestinians just had to sit at home all day. They could not go to school. Palestinians were only allowed out for about half an hour each week to do their shopping.

He believes in peace. 'The Koran calls for peace,' he adds. But he believes peace will only come if Israel gives them the right to education, to travel freely, to be given passports, to be independent, to have their own national identity and their own country. There can be no compromise on these points in his view.

On 14 May 1947 the Zionists declared the State of Israel to exist. The US was quick to recognise this new state.

Armies from surrounding Arab countries attacked but the Israeli forces triumphed and drove Palestinian Arabs from their land. The first Palestinian refugee camps date from this time. The Jews refer to this as the 'Israeli War of Independence'. Palestinian Arabs call it 'The Catastrophe'.

▲ Palestinian refugee camp.

BACKGROUND TO EVENTS FROM THE PALESTINIAN VIEWPOINT

✡ 1947 – Israel is created, backed by the USA and the UN. After the Arab defeat in the war the first Palestinian refugee camps were set up. The Palestinians were forced to leave their land.

Each time the Arab countries fought for the Palestinian cause they were defeated. Inside the camps Palestinians became frustrated with the lack of progress and in 1964 formed their own 'freedom movement', the PLO. In 1968 Yasser Arafat became its leader.

The PLO had few resources so it adopted guerrilla tactics and some factions within it began to commit acts of terrorism. In 1971 they hijacked three airliners. Owing to international pressure the Jordanian government ordered its army to destroy the PLO in Jordan. They were forced out and went to the Lebanon.

✡ 1987 onwards – the Palestinians have launched 'intafadas' or uprisings in the occupied territories.

✡ 1993 – Yasser Arafat and the Israeli Prime Minister, Yitzhak Rabin, shake hands at the White House regarding a peace agreement.

✡ 1994 – a Jewish Zealot kills 29 Arabs in a mosque in Hebron.

✡ 1995 – Yitzhak Rabin is shot dead by a Jewish extremist.

A Palestinian Speaks in 1947

'Britain got our support in the First World War. In return we were promised support in our struggle to win back our country from Turkish rule. The Balfour Declaration is a betrayal by Britain.

The Zionists have been arriving here in their thousands determined to outnumber us and drive us from our farms and businesses. In 1914 they were 8 per cent of the total population. Today this has risen to 36 per cent. We sympathise with the European Jews who have been persecuted and have suffered terribly under the Nazis.

We hope the UN will do better although we are very worried about the US's intentions. Our cause is just. We are happy to live in a democratic Palestine alongside all Jews who lived here before 1914. The rest must go back to Europe.'

Throughout this period the Israelis continued to build settlements in the occupied territories, which the Palestinians consider to be military camps.

The Palestinian Authority set up as a result of the peace process has found it difficult to build a stable government structure, due to a lack of resources and infrastructure.

Following a series of terrorist attacks into Israel from Palestinian territory, the Israelis launched massive military attacks on Palestinian towns and camps to capture the people they blamed for the attack on Israel. This has set the peace process back again and Palestinian factions continue to attack Israeli civilians.

The Palestinians want a homeland with stable borders and most are willing to make an agreement with Israel provided the Israelis withdraw to their former borders and remove their settlements. They also want Jerusalem as their capital city.

GLOSSARY

Intafadas: Palestinian campaign of non cooperation within Israeli controlled areas. Often leading to violence.

Refugees: People who through either fear, violence or natural disaster leave their homes or countries to live temporarily elsewhere.

Questions

1 Why is the issue of the Palestinian refugees so important?
2 Why do the Palestinians want the Israeli settlements removed?
3 How do you think the two peoples could be encouraged to live in peace with each other?
4 How do you think this conflict could be resolved?

Globalisation

Going Shopping – Making Choices

When you go shopping what factors influence your decision to buy one item rather than another?

Name Price BRAND
Availability QUALITY
ENDORSED BY A FAMOUS PERSON

Increasingly citizens want to know more about who makes the products, whether the products are environmentally friendly, what conditions are like for the employees, the manufacturer's reputation, whether child labour is involved in the production, if the production of the goods involved animal tests, if the packaging is recycled or recyclable, whether trees are being replanted.

Many people want to know whether they food they buy is genetically modified (GM), and what additives and preservatives have been used.

▲ Fair Trade goods ensure a fair wage for the worker.

In the past few years there has been a rapid increase in the demand for organic food, that is food produced without any artificial chemical assistance, grown in approved soil conditions.

Below is an example of an organisation trying to promote fair trade.

THE GREENLINE TRADING POLICY

Every effort is made to ensure that all the products sold are:
- People friendly – they do not exploit people in their production and are not unfairly traded. Many products are positively 'fair-traded' giving developing world producers a fair return and support for their communities.
- Animal friendly – they do not involve cruelty in their production or testing.
- Environment friendly – they do not cause excessive damage to the environment. All food products are certified as organic (organically grown), usually by the Soil Association, which tries to operate without using paper. Where this is unavoidable only paper which is 100% recycled is used.

Wherever possible, are goods despatched in re-used packaging, which is collected from a variety of suitable sources and would otherwise be sent to landfill. The use of such packaging does not infer any recommendation of any goods or services advertised thereupon.

 Is this an organisation you would support?
Are you prepared to pay more for their products?

Citizens in the industrialised countries are increasingly demanding higher standards in regard to Fair Trading and Ethical Investment.

Firms such as Body Shop developed and prospered on the basis of the fair trading policies, to such an extent that many major chains of stores are now copying their methods. Alongside these concerns the issue of **globalisation** of world trade and the role of multinationals is an issue for many citizens and numerous pressure groups.

INFO BOX

In the USA, 85 per cent of large companies have **ethical trading** codes of practice. In 1998 the code of conduct movement was launched in the UK.

Marks and Spencer, a leading UK retailer, has an ethical trading policy; they visit their suppliers, seek assurance regarding child labour and working conditions, and work with others to conduct Ethical Trading audits.

EU Demands Ethical Reports

In May 2002 the EU parliament voted to demand that multinational companies publish in their annual reports the social and environmental impact of their businesses.

A recent poll across Europe indicated that 20 per cent of consumers boycott goods on ethical grounds.

GLOSSARY

Boycott: A form of protest involving the non-purchase of goods or services.

Ethical Trading: A system of trading that serves the interests of the producer, retailer and consumer equally. Often linked to codes of conduct covering wages and conditions in manufacturing and production.

Fair Trade: Policy whereby producers receive the best possible price for their products, e.g. small-scale producers of food products.

? Questions

1. Why do you think it is important for companies to have an ethical and fair trade policy?
2. What do you think needs to be done, so that you know more about the goods you are buying?
3. What would cause you to boycott goods?
4. How can you, as a consumer, apply pressure on a large multinational company?

▲ Fair Trade Rally, June 2002, at the House of Commons.

Globalisation

KEY ISSUES
- Are **multinational** companies too powerful?
- Are multinationals accountable?

Who are the Multinationals?

A multinational (or transnational) corporation is a company that operates in more than one country, as opposed to a purely domestic business which has no operations abroad. There are now 63,000 multinational corporations in the world, and between them they are responsible for two-thirds of global trade and 80 per cent of investment. They are the economic force behind globalisation.

As well as basic raw materials from **LEDCs** (Less Economically Developed Countries) that are exported and then processed in other countries, which adds value to the product, concerns have been expressed about the employment of children and the pay and conditions of workers in countries which provide little or no legal protection for workers.

Many multinational companies such as Cadbury Schweppes have introduced Human Rights and Ethical Trading policies so that both workers and customers are aware of 'how our commitment translates into action'.

Cadbury Schweppes – Our Policy

As a responsible corporate citizen, Cadbury Schweppes plc aims to act in a socially responsible manner at all times by: Respecting the economic, social, cultural, political and civil rights of those involved in our operations; Complying with all local human rights legislation; Implementing programmes across our global operations and with our supply chain partners.

Core labour rights and dignity at work
- Preclude the use of forced labour.
- Respect the rights of employees to join legally recognised labour unions.
- Ensure that children are employed only under circumstances that protect them from physical risks and do not disrupt their education.
- Not tolerate any form of harassment in the workplace.

Health and safety in the workplace
- Create a healthy and safe work environment for each employee.

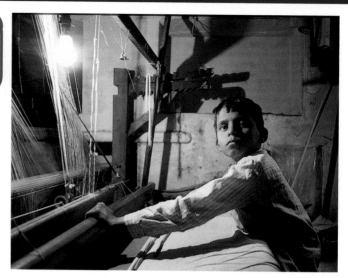

▲ Working conditions for some children are appalling.

Fair remuneration
- Ensure that working hours and remuneration are reasonable and comparable to those offered by similar companies.

Diversity and respect for differences
- Manage diversity to promote and capitalise on cultural and individual differences to create competitive advantage through new perspectives and local market sensitivity.

Opportunity for development
- Recognise the value that employees create and reward them with opportunities for personal and career development.
- Provide employees with equal opportunities regardless of their gender, age, marital status, sexual orientation, disability, race, religion or national origin.

Many pressure groups and others are concerned about how a large number of multinational companies operate. Oxfam Community Aid Abroad demands that companies should allow workers to join trade unions and are paid a full-time wage which allows them to provide for themselves and their families. Independent monitoring systems should be in place to ensure policies are being carried out.

---

i INFO BOX

In Indonesia in July 2002 the entry level full-time wage in a factory making goods for a multinational company was about £1.40 per day.

▲ A closed factory in Yorkshire.

As two women workers in a LDC stated:

'You have to meet the quota before you can go home.' She hit all 15 team leaders in turn from the first one to the fifteenth … the physical pain didn't last long, but the pain I feel in my heart will never disappear.'

Another concern for many countries is the economic power of multinationals in an increasingly global economy.

Factories can be opened or closed, production moved from one country to another. This not only affects the LDCs; in the UK many jobs depend upon the inward and outward movement of investment, which affects jobs. The impact of one of the major

motor car manufacturers moving production from one country to another can have dramatic effects on local communities where they are often the largest employers. The closures or 'down-sizings' also impact on local, regional and national suppliers and sub-contractors to these large firms.

Often manufacturers state they need to move production to enable them to produce goods at a cheaper price, so that they remain competitive and are able to sell their goods.

 What do you think? Is price everything?

Who Controls the Multinationals?

Most multinationals are public companies (plc), accountable for their action to their shareholders. Usually, the larger the company, the larger the number of shareholders. Often a majority of the shares are held by pension funds or other savings institutions on behalf of their investors. Individuals who are shareholders often have very little control of these companies and are out voted by meetings by the institutional shareholders.

GLOSSARY

Globalisation: Ability to produce goods anywhere in the world from materials from anywhere, and sell the product or service anywhere and keep profits in any country.

LDCs: Less Developed Countries. The poorer countries of the world where agriculture is the largest employer. Limited industrial development.

Multinational: A company that operates in several countries producing its goods or offering its services.

▲ The Annual General Meeting (AGM) of a large multinational.

? Questions

1 What are the advantages and disadvantages to a LDC of multinational companies setting up factories in their country?
2 Why are people concerned about the globalisation of world trade?
3 How do you think multinational companies should be made more accountable?

Globalisation

KEY ISSUES

- ○ Foreign Aid – why give it?
- ○ Foreign Debt – keeping the poor poor?
- ○ Can individuals make a difference?

Giving a Helping Hand

▲ Celebrities help to raise funds for people in need.

Through the letter-box, at the door, on television, radio and in the press, voluntary organisations and charities ask for donations to help those abroad who are affected by a natural disaster or facing starvation. Events such as Live Aid and Sport Relief, among others, have raised many millions of pounds to help those in need. The UK government also gives millions of pounds in **foreign aid** each year.

The United Nations has set targets for donor countries of 0.7 per cent of their GNI (Gross National Income) – less than *one* per cent.

Foreign Aid as a % of GNI in 2000	
United Kingdom	0.32%
France	0.32%
Germany	0.27%
Australia	0.27%
Denmark	1.06%
USA	0.10%

Almost all the rich countries of the world have failed to reach this target.

In 2001 the total of world overseas aid declined. In the UK the Chancellor of the Exchequer has

▲ 'How can you refuse?'

promised that the UK will do more to help the poorest countries. The UK has already written off some overseas debts owed to it.

The Weight of Debt

As well as being less developed economically and often suffering from natural disasters and civil unrest, many of the poorer countries are burdened by massive borrowing (foreign loans owed to individual governments or world organisations such as the World Bank).

In 1996 the **OECD** Development Assistance Committee agreed on six measurable targets:
1 Reducing the proportion of people living in extreme poverty.
2 Progress towards universal primary education.
3 More girls in primary and secondary education.
4 Reducing maternal and under 5 mortality.
5 Increasing access to reproductive health services.
6 Reducing loss of environmental resources.

Case Study

Rwanda is one of the poorest countries in the world, with 45 per cent of the population living on less than 60p a day and a GNP (Gross National Product) of 180 US Dollars per head compared to the UK's 18,700 US Dollars. Rwanda owes $1 billion. The burden of paying the interest is a problem. The debt includes nearly $100 million of arrears of interest payments.

In the House of Commons, a committee of MPs has urged that Rwanda have its debts written off so that it can recover economically. What do you think?

▲ Rwanda – one of the poorest countries in the world.

According to the 1997 UNDP Human Development Report: 'relieved of their annual debt repayments, the severely indebted countries could use funds for investments that in Africa alone would save the lives of about 21 million children by 2000 and provide 90 million girls and women with access to basic services.'

Some countries giving foreign aid give it in the form of **credit**, or goods that must be purchased from the donor country. The USA often uses this form of aid. Is it better to give the countries money or credit to buy goods from you? Some countries also use aid as a part of their foreign policies, giving only to their political supporters.

i INFO BOX

AMERICAN FOREIGN AID
While the US aid amount might look very generous in sheer dollar terms, two-thirds of US government aid goes to just two countries: Israel and Egypt. The remaining third is used to promote US exports or to fight the war against drugs.

To reach the target of 0.7 per cent is not an economic problem, but a political one, seen in the context of other spending. For example, the US recently increased its military budget by some $100 billion dollars alone, and Europe subsidises its agriculture and industry even while it demands that other nations liberalise their markets to foreign competition.

'Many in the first world imagine the amount of money spent on aid to developing countries is massive. In fact, it amounts to only .03 per cent of GNP of the industrialised nations. In 1995, the director of the US aid agency said that 84 cents of every dollar of aid goes back into the US economy in goods and services purchased. For every dollar the United States puts into the World Bank, an estimated $2 actually goes into the US economy in goods and services. Meanwhile, in 1995, severely indebted low-income countries paid one billion more in debt and interest to the International Monetary Fund (IMF) than they received from it. For the 46 African countries foreign debt service was four times their combined governmental health and education budgets in 1996. So aid does not aid.'

Jean-Bertrand Aristide, *Eyes of the Heart; Seeking Poor in the Age of Globalisation*, Common Courage Press 2000, p.13

 Do you think this is fair and ethical?

Can we, as individuals make a difference? Bond is a pressure group trying to make a difference. It suggests that as citizens we:
- Write to the Chancellor of the Exchequer.
- Write to the Prime Minister or your MP.

 Do you think it will make a difference?

GLOSSARY

Credits: Money given to countries, but on condition it is spent in the donor country.

Foreign Aid: Money given by government, individuals and organisations to other countries to assist in their development.

OECD: Organisation for Economic Co-operation Development. Body representing the major industrial countries.

? Questions

1. Why do countries give foreign aid?
2. What rules would you draw up regarding the allocation of UK overseas aid?
3. What are the benefits to the rich countries of debt relief?
4. Why are the targets set by the OECD important for LDCs?

KEY ISSUES

○ What problems threaten the world's stability and future?
○ Why are developing countries in so much debt?
○ What is being done to help the poverty stricken?

Many scientists warn that the world's stability and future is threatened because of over-population and the difference in wealth between the rich and developing nations. People in the world's developed countries account for only 20 per cent of the world's population, yet consume 86 per cent of the world's total resources. They own 87 per cent of the world's vehicles, receive over 80 per cent of the world's total income and have most of the world's food. In comparative terms, the rich nations are getting richer and the poor nations are getting poorer. It is becoming more difficult for the poor to make a living and obtain enough food to survive. Many would argue that the events of 11 September 2001, when the planes crashed into the World Trade Center in America, reflect in part the frustration of the 'have-nots' against those who have so much.

How can the people of the developing countries obtain their fair share?

Developing World Debt

Horrendous debt is another major problem facing the developing countries. Debt is having a crippling effect and causing the poor countries to sell off scarce resources. The charity Christian Aid has estimated that poor countries are paying their wealthy lenders around £15 billion every year at a rate of about £40 million a day. Probably three-quarters of this repayment is servicing debts that these countries can never afford to repay. Interest payments on loans use money that could feed the poor and provide a decent standard of living for millions of people. It is estimated that in the continent of Africa, 40 per cent of all government income is spent servicing a total debt of around £225 billion.

Drop the Debt

Many believe that the time has come to write off these enormous debts. **Jubilee 2000** campaigned for the 100 per cent cancellation of all the debts of the developing countries to mark the new millennium. The UK-based lobby group harassed the World Bank and the International Monetary Fund (IMF) for more than five years, asking them and the governments of the wealthy nations to give the world's indebted countries a break. Many believe that it is morally right to help those who are living in absolute poverty and, in addition, that the wealthy nations owe the developing nations because of past exploitations. It is said that between 1503 and 1660, 185,000 kilos of gold and 16 million kilos of silver were taken as plunder from Latin America by Europeans. Britain was among those who raided Africa to take people to use as slaves. Colonists and corporations seized land, labour, minerals and timber in many parts of the world, and compensation has never been paid. Of the **G8** nations, Britain has led the way by writing off millions of pounds of debt owed by the poorest nations.

▲ Jubilee 2000 is supported by many people, including Muhammad Ali, Quincy Jones and Bono (above).

The World Bank

The International Bank for Reconstruction and Development is commonly known as the World Bank. It is a United Nations associate set up to finance projects that further the economic development of its member nations. It has been in existence since 1946 and there are 183 member countries. All members must join the International Monetary Fund. The aim of the IMF is to:

- Promote international monetary cooperation.
- Provide temporary financial assistance to countries to help ease the balance of payments problems.
- Help prevent exchange rates fluctuating wildly.
- Encourage economic growth and high levels of employment.

The United States, Japan, Germany, France and the United Kingdom make the biggest contributions to the World Bank, and so they have the largest say. However, all members are shareholders in the bank. Funds are obtained from three main sources:

- Subscriptions paid by member countries.
- Bond flotations on the world's financial markets.
- Net earnings from the bank's assets.

What Does the Bank Do?

'We share the same world, and we share the same challenge. The fight against poverty is the fight for peace, security, and growth for us all.'

James D. Wolfensohn, President of the World Bank.

After the Second World War, the bank made loans to help rebuild Europe. Gradually the emphasis shifted to helping the developing world. By the end of the 1950s, the bank was issuing loans to help

▲ The World Bank lends countries money to help with such issues as housing and sanitation.

development in Africa, Asia, the Middle East and Latin America. This policy has continued and, for example, during the fiscal year 2000, £12 billion was lent. It is claimed that the bank is working towards a world that is free of poverty, and that it invests money in projects it believes will lead the developing countries towards economic stability. Some of the money goes towards developing the infrastructure of the poorer nations, for example, to provide clean water and sanitation.

GLOSSARY

G8: The world's seven richest nations, plus Russia.

Jubilee 2000: A pressure group which campaigned for the cancellation of all developing world debt to mark the end of the millennium.

▲ The World Bank president, James Wolfensohn.

? Questions

1 What are the dangers if the poor nations continue to get poorer?
2 Explain why developing countries are unable to break free from debt.
3 Do you think that it is reasonable to expect the rich nations to cancel the debt of developing nations? Give reasons for your opinion.
4 Describe the work of the World Bank and the IMF.

KEY ISSUES

○ The problem of population growth.
○ The pressures on the environment.

In recorded history it took until 1830 for the world's population to reach 1 **billion**; by 1930, the world's population had reached 2 billion; by 1960, 3 billion; by 1975, 4 billion; by 1986, 5 billion and in 1999 it reached 6 billion. It is said that the world's population is currently growing at a rate of nearly 80 million a year – it will not be long before 7 billion people inhabit our planet. This is partly because better diet and health care means that people are living longer.

The world is paying a costly environmental and ecological price for this rapid human growth in population. The forests are declining, the topsoil is eroding, the deserts are expanding, and the climate is undergoing radical change. More and more people, desperate to survive, are creating resource shortages. This includes a severe scarcity of water and food in many developing regions.

Over-population Brings Desertification

Scientists warn that much of the world faces an ecological disaster of stunning proportions. The march of the desert sands is accelerating in many areas and water supplies are dwindling.

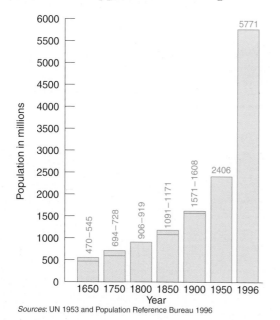

Sources: UN 1953 and Population Reference Bureau 1996

▲ Increase in population 1650–1996.

Desertification is a growing problem in Africa, Asia, Latin America, the Caribbean, and the northern Mediterranean. There is need for action on a global scale and this was stated at a United Nations conference held to consider the problem. Speaking at the conference, German President Johannes Rau estimated that one-quarter of the Earth's surface could turn into desert. He said that approximately 6 million hectares of productive farmland is lost annually to the advance of the deserts, and that around 12 million people die each year because they have not got safe drinking water.

Every African country realises the threat and they are among the 169 countries that have signed up to the United Nations desertification convention. The aim of the convention is to commit countries to fighting desertification at national, sub-regional and regional levels. This will be done by passing laws to protect the environment.

Lake Chad

The dwindling size of Lake Chad, which was one of the largest freshwater lakes in Africa and an important water source in the Sahel, illustrates the problem. Chad, Niger, Nigeria and Cameroon are neighbouring countries of this vast lake and savannah. Lake Chad has the rainforests of the west coast of Africa on one side and the Sahara Desert to the north. Forty years ago the lake covered about 25,000 square kilometres. Now it is one-twentieth of that size, although it does fluctuate according to the season. The annual monsoon rains from June to August provided most of its water, but since the late 1960s, the region has experienced a series of devastating droughts. As a result the region began to undergo desertification.

The situation has worsened because local people have become more dependent on the lake to replace the water they had previously obtained from the monsoons. Overgrazing has led to a drier climate because a lack of vegetation means that the moisture is not recycled back into the atmosphere to the same degree. This has resulted in less monsoon rain and a huge increase in the use of irrigation water from both the lake and the two main rivers that empty into it, the Chari and the Logone. At the same time the Sahara is constantly edging south.

▼ This map shows Lake Chad and Tanzania.

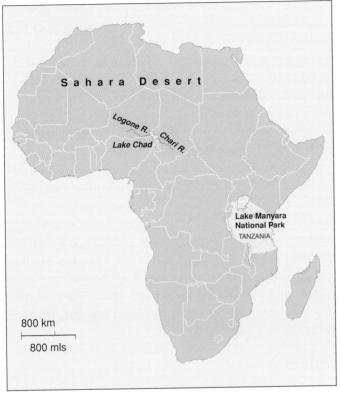

▼ The eland, oryx and kudu are no longer found in Tanzania's national park.

Tanzania

The problem of climatic change also exists in East Africa. When trees are cut down and vegetation overgrazed, the land is unable to retain water and this leads to excessive erosion and exhaustion of surface water and groundwater. Poor cultivation techniques on newly cleared land often exhausts the soil within a few planting seasons, and so more wood is cleared.

This is what has happened in Tanzania. Timber is the country's most important source of energy, accounting for more than 90 per cent of the national energy supply. Farmers also burn large tracts of forest to clear land for crops. The result is vast environmental destruction and the drying up of some of the rivers. Many species of birds, animals and even trees are threatened. It is reported, for example, that eland, oryx, and kudu are no longer found in the Lake Manyara National Park. With more than 400,000 hectares of forests destroyed each year, it is estimated that half the country will be covered by sand within the next 50 years, unless action is taken now.

What can be done? Tanzania's government is encouraging the planting of trees to try to slow down the march of the sands and to limit the environmental damage.

GLOSSARY

Billion: One billion equals 1,000,000,000 or 1 thousand million.

Desertification: The conversion of arid or semi-arid regions to desert due to climatic changes, human activities or both.

? Questions

1 Explain some of the problems resulting from a large growth in population.
2 Why is there a threat to the world from desertification?
3 Explain what is happening to Lake Chad and to Tanzania as a result of pressure from humans.
4 Do you think that anything can be done to reverse the trend and to prevent the expansion of the deserts?

Global Interdependence

KEY ISSUES

○ What is meant by sustainable development?
○ What is Agenda 21?

When travelling around the world by road, rail, boat or plane, planet Earth seems a very large place. Yet, when viewed from outer space our world seems so tiny and insignificant in comparison to the enormous universe. This planet is our only home; it is the only place we know of where the environment and resources can support human life. Billions of people live here and each person's actions have an impact on our world. The growth in population is threatening our future, and 1 billion people are not getting enough to eat. Every 20 minutes, the world adds another 3500 human lives, but it loses one or more entire species of animal or plant life – at least 27,000 species per year.

Currently our major energy source is oil, which is a **finite source**. Once we have used it there will not be any more. The current known supply will last about 20 years. The frequency of discovering new reserves has been decreasing for a long time. Seventy per cent of all developing world families depend upon wood as their sole source of energy, and trees are disappearing at an alarming rate. Action is needed on a global scale to find alternative renewable, non-polluting sources of energy, for example the use of wind, solar, hydro-electric or wave power.

In the last ten years, 1,554000 square kilometres of forest have been cut down. Forests have been described as the lungs of the planet because they turn carbon dioxide into oxygen. Twenty-five years ago lush, majestic trees covered the Himalayan slopes of Nepal. Today those trees are gone and farmers have cut down the underbrush because the growth in population has meant that they are desperate to grow crops. As a result, during the monsoon season precious topsoil has been washed away and the water and topsoil has settled in India, flooding an area the size of Peru and Bolivia. The flooding continues into Bangladesh and brings real disasters to this low-lying country.

Demand on the world's resources is greater than ever before and will continue to grow unless ways can be found to reduce this ever-increasing pressure on our planet. Put simply, future generations will suffer from our selfishness. Many believe that we need to learn to maintain and improve the quality of life and that of future generations by living and acting in a way that is sustainable (can carry on indefinitely). Many people and governments now realise that by providing jobs, homes to live in and ways of travelling, their actions have sometimes had an adverse affect on the environment. For example, we have polluted the air, the land and water with substances which affect our health and which are changing our climate and cause global warming. We are now producing more and more amounts of waste, losing important species and the richness of our wildlife, and using up our natural resources such as freshwater, fuels and minerals. This means that future generations will not have a world with plentiful natural resources or a world that is as pleasant as the one we live in today.

The Brundtland Commission stated in 1987 that we need: *'development which meets the needs of the present without compromising the ability of future generations to meet their own needs.'*

Agenda 21

The United Nations called a meeting in Rio de Janeiro, Brazil in 1992 to discuss new ways of meeting the needs of the world. At this Rio Earth

▲ A mountain of human waste material.

Summit, world leaders discussed how people locally and globally could develop strategies to meet the needs of people in a sustainable way.

Sustainable development means that we provide for people in a way that:
- Looks after the environment.
- Involves everyone in the decisions about our future.
- Is fair to everyone.
- Takes into account the needs of future generations.

Governments pledged to try to do all four of these things at the same time, to improve the quality of life for our world, our future and us. Local, national and international strategies are needed.

At Rio, the world leaders agreed to a global action plan called 'Agenda 21'. This sets out everything that has to be done to promote sustainable development. The conference recognised the need to develop international law to ensure that the delicate balance between the needs for development and for environmental protection is observed.

Local Agenda 21

One of the major proposals was for local councils to work with their communities to devise strategies for meeting their needs in a sustainable way. These plans are called 'Local Agenda 21 Strategies' – in other words 'Local actions for the twenty-first century'.

Dover District Council

Since 1996, Dover District Council has encouraged energy-saving schemes. This has included equipping their council houses with:
- Double-glazed windows.
- New energy-efficient condensing boilers.
- More loft insulation.

The plan to reduce pollution and traffic congestion includes:
- Introducing incentives for car sharing, for example, a car-sharing database.
- Providing more public transport to towns like Deal, Dover and Canterbury.
- Improving facilities for cyclists.
- Providing a cash incentive scheme for people who do not drive to work.
- Encouraging schemes like the walking school bus at Mongeham Primary School. This is like an ordinary bus, with stops and a regular route and timetable. There is one major difference; everyone walks. Parents lead and follow the 'bus' to make sure the children are safe, and children join along the route.

▲ Walking bus schemes are becoming popular around the country.

Recycling is another major feature of Dover's Local Agenda 21. Up to 15,000 pieces of furniture are recycled each year in a scheme that employs six paid employees and a number of volunteer helpers. Bicycles and electrical goods, such as computers, are repaired at a warehouse at Hersden. Unused paint and other items are also recycled.

The Friendship Project has been set up to help people of other nationalities and cultures settle in the area. Local children and asylum seekers have made kites with messages of hope for a peaceful future.

GLOSSARY

Finite sources: These sources are limited and are not being replaced, and so they will run out, e.g. oil supplies.

Sustainable development: Development that meets the needs of the people today, without compromising the ability of future generations to meet their own needs.

? Questions

1. Explain the difference between a finite source and a renewable source.
2. Explain what is meant by sustainable development.
3. What is Agenda 21, where did it originate and what does it set out to do?
4. How can global issues be addressed by local action?
5. Outline some of Dover District Council's Local Agenda 21 action plans.

KEY ISSUES

○ What can be done to bring about sustainable development in the world?
○ How can individuals help?

Making a Difference

The human race is in great danger of destroying not only modern civilisation but also all life itself. This is because we have:

- Exploited the earth's resources with no regard for the consequences.
- Eroded the ozone layer which protects all life on earth from dangerous ultraviolet rays.
- Polluted the air, water and land with poisons, pesticides and gases which cause global warming.
- Created nuclear bombs and other weapons of mass destruction.
- Created an unparalleled population explosion.
- Allowed the gap between the very rich and the very poor (both among and within nations) to grow and grow.
- Allowed an enormous concentration of power to develop in the hands of a few.
- Allowed a growing resentment and frustration amongst many, which may be shown in the spread of terrorism.

The world leaders stated at the Rio Earth Summit in 1992 that the situation requires action on a global scale. This means **thinking globally**, but **acting locally**. Every area in the global community needs to take action that will encourage sustainable development. Whatever the local need or issue, consideration needs to be given to the impacts on other communities and their environment. Agenda 21 makes it unacceptable, for example, for councils in northern England to give planning permission for factories, which send pollution into the atmosphere and cause acid rain in Scandinavia and Germany, and global warming. However, the issues go beyond protecting the environment. It is important to examine both the economic systems that provide jobs and income for people, and the political systems which make decisions about how social and economic systems use natural resources. Agenda 21 has made national governments and local authorities develop their own plans for sustainable development. These are based on local needs and on the development of partnerships between all sectors of the community, such as businesses, voluntary groups and young people.

What Is Being Done?

Since 1992 many schemes have developed to fulfil the criteria laid down by Agenda 21. For example, in West Africa over 11 million people depend on cocoa production for their livelihood. Concerned about **deforestation**, disease and soil erosion, members from the chocolate industry, researchers, conservationists, growers and economists met at the Smithsonian Tropical Research Institute in Panama in 1998. They tried to determine what sustainable cocoa production should be like. Their main conclusions were that cocoa farming:

- Has an important role to play in many of the rural economies of West Africa.
- Has the potential to be used as a conservation tool.
- Needs research to give small farmers environmentally-friendly disease and pest control tools.
- Needs improvement programmes and research into creating a canopy of other trees to create a diversified agroforestry system.

By using this information in countries like Cote d'Ivoire, legume trees are now being planted to protect young cocoa trees. This is important because Cote d'Ivoire had one of the fastest deforestation rates in the world.

▲ Cocoa pods.

CAMPFIRE, Zimbabwe

CAMPFIRE (Communal Areas Management Programme for Indigenous Resources) is a programme designed to help rural development and conservation in parts of Zimbabwe. It is based on sustainable and appropriate ways of using the wildlife and of managing the arid and semi-arid communal lands (42 per cent of the country). Five main schemes have been carefully developed:

- Leasing trophy hunting concessions to foreign hunters who come to Zimbabwe to hunt elephants, buffaloes, lions or other wild animals.
- Harvesting natural resources. Communities sell a limited number of natural products, such as crocodile eggs, timber, river sand and caterpillars.
- Tourism. Local people provide basic facilities and act as guides. Schemes, such as bird-watching and access to natural hot springs, are being developed.
- Live animal sales. Where there is a high wildlife population some are sold to National Parks or Game Reserves.
- Selling meat. Some meat is sold if the animals are plentiful.

CAMPFIRE has created jobs, provided the incentive to conserve wildlife and generated finance for the local people.

What Can Individuals Do?

No doubt you will have heard the phrase that 'every little helps'. Some ideas that have been suggested for sustainable development are:

- Reduce family sizes by using family planning methods.
- Adopt or sponsor a child in a developing country.
- Support charities that are developing sustainable projects in the developing countries.
- Encourage involvement in the community.
- Encourage spending on education.
- Ride a bike or walk to your destination if that is possible. On longer journeys use public transport or if that is not possible use cars that are energy efficient.
- Pick up rubbish and do not litter the environment.
- Encourage the planting of trees.
- Recycle goods and create compost from perishable rubbish.
- Use alternative forms of energy (e.g. solar).
- Campaign for people to become more aware of the need for sustainable development, for example, write to newspapers, councillors or MPs.

▲ Wildlife in Zimbabwe.

GLOSSARY

Think global, act local: Phrase from the Rio Conference that aimed to get local communities working together on environmental issues to made a global impact

Deforestation: Clearing vast areas of the world's trees to gain the available timber and to provide agricultural land. This has often led to the cleared land losing the ability to grow crops because of erosion and the loss of nutriments.

? Questions

1 Explain how human actions threaten the existence of life on earth.
2 How can global issues be addressed by local action?
3 Describe a scheme in West Africa which is encouraging sustainable development.
4 How is CAMPFIRE helping the people in the rural communities of Zimbabwe?
5 What local action plans for sustainable development (Local Agenda 21) and priorities have been set by your local authority?
6 Explain some of the actions that individuals could take to help promote sustainable development.

Sustainable Development and Local Agenda 21

Case Study

KEY ISSUES

- How do we resolve starvation?
- Can world health be improved?
- Does the media report the development and use of GM foods accurately?
- Why are people concerned about GM foods?

Genetically Modified Foods

Genetic modification within food production is attracting a great deal of attention. The debate about genetically modified (GM) foods raises many issues, including those of a scientific, environmental, social, technological, ethical and political nature.

What is Genetic Modification?

Genes are the building blocks of life – every plant, animal and human is a product of their genes.

Genes are not static and with each new generation of plan, genes are 'modified' naturally to create new biological variants. Genetic modification is simply an extension of what happens in nature.

At its simplest, plants have been modified through **selective breeding** to meet consumer demand, for example:

- Potatoes are native to America but are now grown in Europe.
- Apples are grown for taste, texture, colour and to be of a specific size.
- Carrots are grown to be straight and larger.

Currently genetic modification involves selecting a specific gene and introducing it into another plant. For instance:

- 'Calgene's Flavr Savr' tomatoes have been modified to slow down the rate of ripening.
- Oil seed rape has been modified to produce soap at a very economical price.

The Arguments Against GM Foods
Are GM Foods Safe?

The view of those who are against GM foods is that more independent testing needs to be carried out for the public to have confidence in genetic modification.

The Impact of GM Foods on the Environment

1 Insect-resistant crops may damage species of wildlife, for example, butterflies.
2 The insects that GM crops are designed to kill, may become resistant to the crops. This could lead to farmers using chemical sprays to control the insects.
3 Research is needed to investigate the potential transfer of genes from GM crops to other crops which could result in either super weeds (i.e. weeds resistant to control methods) or the contamination of non-GM crops. This would remove the diversity of crops and growth in organic farming.

The Arguments for GM Foods
Could GM foods reduce world starvation?

1 World food production can be increased. Genetic modification allows plants to be grown in previously inhospitable climates. For example, a corn plant could be modified to grow using less water and could be grown in a desert climate. This would reduce starvation in developing countries.
2 GM crops can ensure that food production keeps pace with population growth. The last dramatic increase in food production came with the use of **fertilisers**, irrigation and **pesticides**. However, these methods cannot produce enough food to keep up with the increase in populations without severe environmental damage, whereas GM foods can.

▲ Crop spraying by plane.

Could GM foods solve certain health problems?

1 Plants could be genetically modified to increase nutritional value. For example, 'golden rice' a vitamin A enriched rice developed to stop blindness (due to vitamin A deficiency) in the developing world.

2 Plants could be modified so that their fruit contained antibiotics or **vaccines** – you could eat strawberries and obtain immunity to measles.

Other Considerations

GM foods can actually ease the negative impact that agriculture has on the environment. For example, insect-resistant crops enable farmers to reduce the amount of insecticide they use. Plants have been developed that take in toxic substances such as TNT and mercury from ex-Army sites. These plants either break down the chemicals and release them as harmless substances, or they take in the chemicals and use them to grow.

Politics

The verdict of a House of Lords committee stated that the potential benefits of GM foods far outweighed the risks.

What stance therefore should the British government take?

INFO BOX

These headlines have been used in relation to GM foods:

FRANKENSTEIN FOODS

STOP GM FOODS

Terminator Genes

▲ Protestor destroying a GM crop.

The Media

The media widely reports the negative side of GM foods and the action taken by GM protestors, but seldom indicates the usefulness of GM foods. It is therefore difficult for the public to know the facts.

GLOSSARY

Fertilisers: Chemicals added to the soil to improve crop fertility.

Pesticides: Chemicals sprayed on animals and plants to stop the spread of diseases.

Selective breeding: A traditional means of improving the quality of livestock or plants by cross-breeding different varieties.

Vaccines: A substance made from germs that gives an individual a mild form of a disease in order for them to build up a resistance to the disease.

? Questions

1 What are the main public concerns relating to GM foods?
2 Why should we continue to research and use GM foods?
3 Do protestors have the right to damage crops and if so why?
4 Explain how developing countries might gain from GM crops.
5 Do GM crops get a fair hearing in the press?

Case Study

What Price Petrol?

KEY ISSUES

○ Who controls oil prices?
○ How can a pressure group react?
○ What are the environmental costs?
○ What are the alternatives?

The Energy Crisis – a Global Problem

In 2002, **fossil fuels** accounted for 88 per cent of the world's energy use, we are using fossil fuels at a greater rate than they can be naturally created. It took 1 million years to create the resources we are rapidly consuming today.

The Energy Crisis – a UK Problem

The population of the UK are major consumers of fossil fuels. We believe that we have the right to drive our cars almost anywhere, from city centres to the remote countryside. We take it for granted that petrol will be available at our local petrol station.

Do We Pay too Much for Our Petrol?

In 1965 you could buy 5 litres of petrol for £1. In 2002 the cost is close to £4. For every £50 worth of petrol you put into a car's petrol tank, the government takes £37 in taxes. The actual production cost of a litre of petrol is 22.8p, but an added 61.4p **fuel duty** and VAT goes to the government. The production cost of petrol has not always increased so rapidly, as the following chart shows.

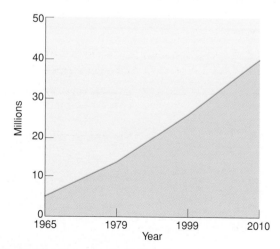

▲ The number of cars on the UK roads.

▼ Petrol costs 1965–2000

Date	Cost and profit/litre	Government taxes/litre	Pump prices/litre
1965	14.0p	39.5p	53.5p
1979	13.9p	47.8p	61.7p
1999	13.1p	58.1p	71.2p
2000	22.8p	61.4p	84.2p

So Why Have Pump Prices Increased?

Why does the government tax fuel to this extent? One implication of high fuel prices is that all road transportation costs increase. British haulage companies face financial hardship and certainly cannot compete favourably with their European competitors who have the advantage of cheaper fuel.

Who Controls Oil Production Costs?

OPEC (The Organisation of Petroleum Countries) has 11 members who have agreed to keep prices at around $22–28 **a barrel**. They control production levels so that the market does not have a surplus of oil to trade. Some oil-producing countries like the UK and USA choose not to join OPEC.

Petrol prices have much to do with politics at the international level and here in Britain. In the crisis of 2000 petrol prices were rising due to the huge amount of tax levied on our petrol and people were determined to have their voices heard. Protests quickly brought the nation to a virtual standstill. A pressure group developed national support. It became known as the 'Dump the Pump' campaign.

There are also Environmental Costs

Date:	24 March 1989. Time 00.04
Place:	Blight Reef, Prince William Sound – 25 miles from Port Valdez in Alaska
Ship:	Exxon Valdez (oil tanker)
Cargo:	53 million gallons of crude oil

The Exxon Valdez ran aground and within eight hours, 11.2 million gallons of the crude oil it was carrying had spilled into Prince William Sound, Alaska. A total of eight of the 11 cargo holds were ripped open along almost the entire length of the 300-m hull.

Damage Done

The oil dispersed over a distance of 756 km. Forty per cent of spilled oil was deposited in Prince William Sound, causing devastation to the **ecosystem**. A 2092-km stretch of coastline was oiled.

Cause of the Disaster

At the time the Exxon Valdez went aground, there was no Senior Officer on the bridge, the Captain was suspected of being drunk and failed to provide a proper navigation watch. The Third Mate failed to manoeuvre the vessel safely, due to fatigue from excessive workload. (Source: adapted from the National Transport Safety Board Marine Accident Report.)

In 2002, 20 per cent of the oil spill still remained along the Alaskan coastline.

The Local Economy and Ecosystem

The local economy relied very heavily on fishing and will be devastated for years. The ecosystem may never fully recover. Around 35,000 sea birds and over 3000 sea otters were cleaned and survived. Many thousands perished and sank. Eighty-five per cent of Alaska's economy is dependent on oil. The US and Alaskan governments introduced the 1990 Oil Pollution Act to bring new laws into force on the transportation of crude oil.

The Future

To reduce the use of fossil fuels for transport, the UK needs to develop better public transport systems to encourage car owners to use the rail networks and local public transport.

Alternative Energy Sources

There are a number of alternative sustainable energy sources, which include: wind power, wave power, solar power, hydroelectric power and liquid petroleum gas (LPG). It is possible to use solar power and LPG to power the family car.

Are Gas-Powered Cars the Future

LPG is half the cost of conventional petrol and most normal cars can be converted to run on it. In addition, the emissions are less harmful. The government has extended its programme to help motorists with the cost of converting to gas.

In other countries LPG is more common. All of the taxis in Tokyo run on autogas. In Italy more than 1 million cars accept gas. In Britain the figure is more like 50,000 and many of these are duel-fuel vehicles that accept gas as well as petrol.

GLOSSARY

A barrel of oil: Is the standard measure used in the oil industry, equal to 191 litres. The average US citizen consumes the equivalent of 22 barrels of oil a year.

Eco system: A term used to describe the total environmental system that exists in a given area.

Fossil fuels: Decomposed animal and plant life from millions of years ago, that has been transformed into gas and liquid fuels.

Fuel duty: A special tax charged by the government on fuels. Different levels apply to different types of fuel.

? Questions

1 Why should we be concerned about our use of fossil fuels?
2 What arguments are there for the government to increase or decrease the level of fuel tax?
3 Why should polluters pay for the damage they cause?

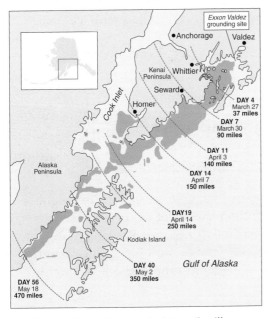

▲ This map shows the extent of the oil spill.

Case Study

The Future Citizen

KEY ISSUES

○ What issues face society today and what are we likely to face in the future?
○ How important is it to be an **active citizen**?

Back to the Past?

What sort of world will it be in 2080? How will you explain to your grandchildren how our society and world is organised and run?

Is This What It Is Going To Be Like?

Life and the way we organise ourselves, and participate in our society is constantly changing. Just think about what changes took place in the twentieth century. By 2080 what issues are likely to have been tackled?

Is there a future for our schools? In the age of ICT all of your learning can take place wherever you choose. You might only need to meet others to enjoy leisure activities.

What sort of work will be available? Will all factories be largely automated? Will people work mainly from home using computers? Will there be a large increase in low-skilled, domestic and caring work?

Life itself will be longer if the past is a predictor; already governments are discussing the idea of people working until 70 plus to pay for their pensions. What will life be like for you as a fit and mentally alert 100-year-old person? What impact will medical advances have on our society? What moral and ethical issues will they raise and how will they be resolved?

▲ A world with environmental problems, at war with itself and the end of the traditional workplace?

Will government be closer to the people? Could there be a regular TV slot where citizens can vote on issues affecting their communities? Will those elected be closer to the citizen by an instant means of communication?

Will the current boundaries that we call countries exist by 2080? Will the UK be part of a United States of Europe with a directly elected Head of State? Will national government have disappeared? After 600 years will the **nation-state** be an old-fashioned idea?

By 2080, will we have resolved the issue of a rich one-third of the world and a poor two-thirds, the overfed and the underfed? Will we still be concerned about what we eat and how it is produced? Will the multinational companies have grown even more powerful, more powerful than governments or bodies such as the European Union and the United Nations?

Will the idea of war be out of date? Will the causes of terrorism be resolved? Will world government through the United Nations be strengthened? The issues of the environment and our use of our scarce resources – will they have been solved?

Every generation looks back as well as forward. If you speak to an elderly person they will tell how how much society has changed since they were young people of your age. Things you take for granted either did not exist or had not been invented. Can you imagine life without television, a computer or a mobile phone? Travelling any distance used to mean a train journey; visiting the doctor or the dentist was not free – there was a bill to pay. Holidays were, at most, a week by the seaside in the UK and fresh vegetables were something you grew in your own garden.

The future is determined by the citizens of today and tomorrow. This book has addressed the themes of rights and responsibilities, power and authority and decision making, as they are today.

What are a citizen's basic rights, what responsibilities do we have to the community and the society to which we belong? Who should exercise power over our lives and to whom should that person be accountable? Who has the right to know about our lives – will freedom of information mean access to any piece of information held by anybody? How should we arrive at decisions? Do we merely vote every four or five years, elect politicians, and let them get on with it? Or should a citizen be more **active**, questioning and demanding that those in power are held to **account**, and that the citizens' views are considered?

What sort of society do you want to pass on to your grandchildren? Do not forget to ask your grandparents what they thought the future held for you.

GLOSSARY

Accountability: The idea of those in authority having responsibility for those who have given them that authority, i.e. those elected and the electorate, company officials and their shareholders.

Active citizenship: A description of a citizen in a modern state who fully participates in the society through the democratic process.

Nation-state: A political and legal structure based upon agreed physical boundaries that grants those living within its boundaries the rights of citizenship. This dates from the late middle ages.

Passive citizenship: A description of a citizen who does not participate or question the processes of society, or only takes part in a limited way, e.g. occasionally votes.

Questions

1 What sort of society do you want to pass on to your grandchildren?
2 What do you think are a citizen's basic human rights?
3 i) What issues and problems do you think will be unresolved in 2080?
  ii) What issues and problems do you think will have been resolved by 2080?
  iii) Give reasons for your choices in i) and ii).
4 Why do you think it is better to have a society made up of active rather than passive citizens?

Examination Preparation

AQA GCSE Citizenship (short course) involves a written examination and coursework. The examination is worth 60 per cent of the marks (the coursework is worth 40 per cent). The examination is 1 hour and 30 minutes long.

The more demanding exam questions require a detailed response. The examiners will mark these questions using a levelled mark scheme (the better the answer, the higher the level obtained and therefore the higher the mark – rather like climbing the rungs on a ladder). See later examples on page 116.

The Question Paper has Four Sections

Section A has approximately 15 short-answer questions and each question is worth 2 marks. The questions are drawn from all three topic areas of your course:

Topic 1 – School and Work and Local Community
Topic 2 – National and European Citizenship
Topic 3 – Global Citizenship

It is possible to gain 1 mark for a partially correct answer or 2 marks for a correct answer. Remember, a wide range of knowledge specific to the course is required to do well in this section. A detailed answer is not expected for a 2-mark question. The space available on the paper will be limited to two or three lines per question.

Section B contains a stimulus response question, which will focus on a specific community-based issue selected by the examination board.

You are required to read the source and answer one question, which will be subdivided into a number of parts. The stimulus material could relate to any part of the course.

Read the source material at least twice. By referring to the source material you will be able to answer the first part of the question; subsequent questions will require the 'use of the source and your own knowledge' to be answered fully.

The range of marks possible for each question progressively increases, and so your answers will need to become more detailed as you answer each question. You will be given more space for the questions offering higher marks. Use the space as a guide for the amount you need to write.

You must obtain some detail from the source in the examination paper and fully develop your response using knowledge gained from classroom studies or background reading. This will enable you to produce answers that are relevant, detailed and in some depth. Full explanations with specific examples will clearly gain more marks and place your work at the highest level. Full marks can be obtained for answers that are both specific and relevant to the task; these can include real life situations, which support your answer.

Section C will ask questions that are specific to a practical citizenship activity that you have undertaken. You may wish to refer to your coursework. A series of questions will seek knowledge and understanding of the various stages you went through. For example, planning your involvement and contribution, the views, opinions and contributions of others, whether the activity was successful and the lessons learned. It would be very helpful to retain a copy of your coursework, to read again prior to the examination.

In **Section D** you are asked to answer one question from a choice of three. The question requires a short essay-style response and each is worth a total of 30 marks. The three questions to choose from will cover the three themes of citizenship.

Theme 1 – Rights and Responsibilities
Theme 2 – Decision Making, Power and Authority
Theme 3 – Participation in Citizenship Activities and the three topics in the specification.

An additional supportive framework will be offered in the examination paper to help you to focus your answer on the task set. These prompts will help you with the structure of your essay. You will not be penalized if you do not use the framework.

Finally, 6 additional marks are available for 'written communication': make sure that your spelling, punctuation and grammar are accurate and use a suitable style of writing.

Examples of the Type of Questions in Section A

Example 1
Q1 Name two ways you can participate in the electoral system when you are 21 years old (2 marks) Because this is a 2-mark question, you would gain 1 mark for each correct response, up to a maximum of 2 marks, for example:
- Vote at a recognised polling station.
- Stand for election as a candidate.
- Become an election agent.

Example 2
Q1 What is meant by a 'multicultural society?' (2 marks) Because this is also a 2-mark question, your response to gain full marks should indicate that: A multicultural society comprises people from a variety of cultures, nations and ethnic backgrounds. 1 mark would be awarded if only 'cultures', 'variety of nations' or 'ethnic backgrounds' was given.

Example 3
Q1 What does CRE stand for? (2 marks) If you gave the answer as the 'Commission for Racial Equality' you would gain full marks. 1 mark would be awarded for an almost correct understanding.

Examples of the Type of Questions in Section B

Example 4 is about participation and community issues. You may be given source material as illustrated below.

The Weekly News

The local Health Trust announced today that the accident and emergency unit at the Teemouth hospital will close in three months. The unit will be transferred to a larger hospital in the neighbouring town of Exton, some 15 miles away.

Local Council Leader Jean Smith said that the council would fight to keep the unit open.

Local MP Heather George, speaking from London, declared that she intended to join the fight to keep the accident and emergency unit open.

The questions asked regarding this source could require you to:
- Outline the nature of the issue affecting the community.
- Find out who else other than the local council and the MP could be involved in campaigning to keep the unit open.
- Decide what methods a campaign group could use to persuade the Health Trust to change its mind and which are likely to be the most successful.

The questions in **Section C** refer to the citizenship activity in which you have been involved. Therefore, keep a copy of your final report and re-read it before your examination to refresh your memory of:
- The activity undertaken.
- The planning stages.
- The involvement of yourself and others.
- The final evaluation of the participative citizenship activity, so that you are familiar with its structure.

The response to the question does not have to be based upon your submitted coursework task. It could be based upon any citizenship activity you have undertaken.

You will be asked to briefly outline the nature of your citizenship activity. Your answer will give the examiner an understanding of your activity and your subsequent responses. Questions may include the following:

Q1 Outline the planning that took place before the activity began (5 marks)
Answer: What did you plan to do and what planning did other people undertake? A step-by-step plan of what you intended to undertake would be an ideal answer. Indicate the process you went through, the strategies you used, the aims and objectives of the activity, all clearly related to the information given in Question 1. This would be worth full marks.

Q2 Following the outline planning stage, detail your own contribution (5 marks)
Answer: At this stage indicate in detail what *you* did and the contribution *you* made to the activity. Indicate the strengths and weaknesses of *your* contribution.

Q3 Indicate the contribution made by other people associated with your citizenship activity and compare their contribution with your contribution (10 marks)

Answer: Detail what other people (peer group) did.

- List the contribution of older people (e.g. school staff).
- In what way(s) did people gain from the activity?
- Compare, contrast and finally evaluate the contribution of other people.
- Indicate their strengths and weaknesses.

Q4 Indicate the success of the activity, what lessons were learned and what improvements can be made for the future continuation and development of the activity (15 marks)

Answer:

Level 1 (the first rung on the ladder) – very brief account of the activity. Few clear points given about the success of the activity (1–3 marks).

Level 2 (second rung of the ladder) – you will already have achieved Level 1 and you should now add an outline of the activities' success at a basic level. Some of the lessons learned should be included (4–6 marks).

At Level 3 (having already achieved Level 2) you will further develop the lessons learned and the improvements that could be made in the future. A logical and structured framework indicating your clear understanding of the question should be given (7–9 marks).

At Level 4 an account that indicates the success of the activity, logically presented and supported by evidence, is required. Improvements to the planning stage and progress of the activity and how it could have been improved should be offered (10–12 marks).

At Level 5, to obtain the highest level and gain the full marks available, your response should give a full and detailed indication of the lessons learned and the improvements that could be made. The points made should be logical and fully supported by the evidence given. Planning and progress are linked, improvements are offered through the experiences gained and evaluations made. Suggested improvements are within the framework of the task, the resources and time available.

In **Section D** you must answer only one question from a choice of three.

One question will be on 'Rights and Responsibilities', the next on 'Decision Making, Power and Authority' and the final question will be on 'Participation in Citizenship Activities'. Each will be based upon one of the three topics in the specification.

Each question is worth 30 marks – but remember you only have to answer ONE question.

The good news is that you will be given the title of the essay and a number of prompts to help you focus on the task set.

Examples of questions include:

Rights and Responsibilites

Q1 Many people talk about their rights. Do pupils and teachers have rights and responsibilities in schools? (30 marks)
You might like to include basic legal rights:
- Mention the Human Rights Act at the European Convention.
- You might indicate that rights also bring responsibilities that affect you and your teachers.
- Give examples of rights and responsibilities that affect you and your teachers.

Decision Making, Power and Authority

Q2 Who has the authority to make decisions in your school? (30 marks)
You might like to:
- Include individuals who exercise power and authority in school.
- Include groups who exercise authority.
- Indicate how schools provide opportunity for 'pupil power'.

Participation in Citizenship Activities

Q3 Why do people prefer to join pressure groups rather than political parties? (30 marks)
You might like to include:
- The meaning of the term pressure groups.
- The difference between political parties and pressure groups.
- Why pressure group activities attract more interest than those of political parties. The answer will be supported by contemporary examples.

Remember – the supportive framework offered with each question is to give you some help. You do not need to follow this guidance, you can offer your own structure and approach to answer the question.

How to Gain Full Marks

The questions in **Section D** will also be marked on 6 Levels of response. Level 1 is a very basic response, while Level 6 will only be achieved by a very detailed account that fully answers the questions.

The responses for the questions above are marked as follows for each level:

- Level 1 answer – contains one or two points that are relevant. A poor descriptive account is given. (1–5 marks)
- Level 2 – a partial answer that contains several relevant points but is largely descriptive in nature. (6–10 marks)
- Level 3 answer – most of the main points are covered in a structured way. Some points are fully developed, many are not. Some examples are given. Limited evaluations and conclusions are given. (11–15 marks)
- Level 4 answer – covers all the main points of the

question. The response has a clear structure and includes examples. Some evaluation is given. (16–20 marks)
- Level 5/6 answers – a logical structured account is offered, covering all the main points which are supported by examples and evidence. Sound evaluation and clear conclusions are given in an integrated way. (Level 5 11–25 marks; Level 6 26–30 marks)

 INFO BOX

TO SUCCEED IN THIS EXAMINATION YOU SHOULD DO THE FOLLOWING:
- Study the structure of the paper.
- Read your Practical Citizenship coursework prior to the examination.
- Familiarise yourself with the content of this book.

i INFO BOX

HOW TO MAKE THE EXAMINER'S LIFE EASY
- Write legibly so the examiner can read your answer easily.
- Make sure your answers flow in a logical order.

Coursework Guidance

KEY ISSUES

- ○ Select an activity that you really wish to participate in and get fully involved with.
- ○ Be an active citizen taking real responsibility to help others.
- ○ Plan what you intend to do carefully.
- ○ Write a report based on your activity.

A Challenge or an Opportunity?

Coursework is an essential part of the GCSE Citizenship (short course) examination. You will have to produce one piece of coursework of approximately 2000 words in length. Coursework will count for 40 per cent of the total marks for the whole course.

Introduction

Your coursework must relate to your active participation within a school or the wider community. At this stage the more active your involvement the better. Desk-bound research will not be enough, although you may need to do some research to help produce a well-rounded piece of original work. You will need to give careful thought to the activity before, during and after its completion to ensure that you are able to demonstrate:
- Skills of active participation.
- Responsible action.
- Gaining knowledge and understanding relevant to citizenship.

A written report is required and you can write your report stage by stage as you undertake the activity. The final evaluation and conclusions should be written towards the end of the course. This will give you the opportunity to reflect on your work. Further ideas and examples are given on the next page.

Report Format

As you become actively involved and research your coursework, you may obtain and process a range of data, evidence and information. This may include:

- Questionnaire results.
- A case study.
- Survey findings.
- Interviews.
- Records of debates or speeches.
- Information from books.
- Letters that you have written.
- Records of visits that you have made.

Above all, you must become actively involved and participate as a responsible citizen.

> Collect ideas → Start thinking → Start planning

Stage 1 – The Plan

- Outline what your citizenship activity is about and how it relates to this Citizenship Studies course.
- Write a brief introduction and discuss this with your teachers. Can you justify the activity?
- Is the activity school based or based in the wider community? Will you do it alone, in a group or in a combination of the two?
- Now list what you think you need to do in order to complete the coursework.
- Check with your teacher, discuss a structure and begin to develop an **Action Plan**. Remember:

1 To list the various stages.
2 To list the intended outcomes.
3 To list what practical things you and others will need to do.
4 To think about how much time you will give to the activity.

Careful planning is the key at this stage.

Stage 2 – The Activity

You will need to write up an account of the citizenship activity – so keep all your rough notes. Keep a diary of what you do or plan to do:

- Indicate what, when, where and how you become involved.

- Say what you actually did.
- Say what other people your age, younger and older than you, did.
- Explain what roles and relationships you and others had.
- Indicate the rights and responsibilities you and others had.
- Show what research you did and why.
- Note what information was easy to obtain, who gave it to you and what was useful (be selective).
- Write it up; give your opinions, draw conclusions from what you have learned.

> - Do not undersell yourself – if you were fully involved in the citizenship activity, say so!
> - Say whether it was a five-day activity, as in Work Experience, or 30 minutes every day for a term or once a week.
> - Say if it is a fund-raising event that involves you at various times of the day, evening or at weekends.

HAS THAT MADE YOU THINK?

Stage 3 – The Evaluation

After the activity is undertaken you need to write it up, including the Planning Stage and the Activity Stage. The Evaluation Stage is last, but it is still very important.

You will need to draw together your opinions and conclusions, clearly stating:

- Your role, your views, your experience and the contribution you have made.
- The roles, views, experience and contributions of *other* people involved in the citizenship activity.
- Opinions and conclusions, reflections on the activity, its value to others, the planning and strategies you adopted (did they help you to achieve the initial aim?).
- What you learned, and what you and others gained from undertaking the activity.
- What changes you would recommend that would have 'improved' the activity.

> **Reminder** – the word limit is 2000 – you may need to re-draft and use an appendix if your report is too long.

Resources List

Your activity may have involved gathering information from a variety of sources. All the resources you have used should be written on the resources list, which should be attached to your coursework report.

Ideas for Coursework

The practical citizenship activity may be selected from within the subject content of this book. It may be school based, work based or based within the local community – Topic 1. It could be based on Topic 2 – national and European citizenship issues or criminal and civil law. Finally, it could be based on Topic 3 – global issues. Think of global issues and how you could act locally to improve the quality of life for others.

The most important thing is that you must enjoy, value and be actively involved in the activity. The most important decision you will make is the first one! Choose the activity you really want to do. Negotiate this with your teachers.

Ideas for your Coursework Task

After talking to your teacher, you may decide to base your activity within school and to go it alone or work with other pupils (a whole-class activity is a possibility). Or you may decide to work in an active way in the wider community outside school. Look again at the work you have undertaken from this book and consider the following ideas. Then discuss the advantages and disadvantages of them before finally deciding on your active citizenship activity.

Topic 1: Ideas
- Consider exploring the roles and responsibilities of employees and employers within your work experience placement.
- Consider how you could bring about change in your community. This could involve coaching young people in sport, helping to regenerate a local problem area or pressing the council into action on a local issue.
- Work on a reading programme with younger students each week to improve their learning.

Topic 2: Ideas
- Think about a topical national or European issue, and investigate ways that you can get involved at a local level (e.g. it could be a political or environmental issue).
- Participate in a national organization that operates locally (e.g. Child Line) or organize a local activity and be part of a national event (e.g. Red Nose Day).
- Organize a mock election or local debating society.
- A national event is often reported differently by different sections of the media – you could canvass public opinion locally and report your findings.
- Think about school rules and how they might be changed for the better, e.g. can you influence a reduction in graffiti in school?

Topic 3: Ideas
- Does your school have contacts abroad? Can you take part in a cultural exchange or work abroad in your holidays helping on a community project?
- Help to organise a visiting speaker to address your group on a global issue.
- Get involved in a global environmental issue at a local level, e.g. recycling or reducing pollution.

How Will the Coursework Be Assessed?

When undertaking your coursework it is useful to know how it will be assessed. It helps you to plan ahead and to pick up maximum marks as you go along. Remember these **key points**.

Your work will be assessed on the following:
- How well you plan your citizenship activity.
- How well you carry out the activity and how actively involved you are.
- Your knowledge and understanding of the citizenship activity.
- How well you obtain and explain the information you collect.
- How well you express your opinions and draw conclusions.
- How well you evaluate your work.

Marks Will Be Awarded for

Stage 1 – Planning

Plan carefully:
- Is the task clearly based upon the specification?
- Do you show a 'real' sense of purpose?
- Does the activity have a value to other people?
- Have you clearly thought through what needs to be done?
- Do you need to undertake any additional research?

The key is to plan carefully and to consider any problems you may encounter. Remember that you have a limited amount of time to complete the coursework.

Stage 2 – The Activity (Part 1)

(I) Knowledge and understanding:
- Can you clearly show the knowledge and understanding that you have gained?
- Can you display an understanding and insight into the roles, relationships and rights of *everyone* involved in the activity, including your own, those of others who have helped you and the people who have benefited from the activity?

The key is how much knowledge and understanding you have gained from the activity itself, and from researching the wider issues of the activity.

Stage 2 – The Activity (Part 2)

(II) Explanation and interpretation of the evidence collected:
- You must gather, summarise and present a wide range of information and data, and present it effectively in your written report.
- You may offer some background research.
- You need to give opinions and draw conclusions based on the above.
- Make sure you keep a diary of everything you do.

The key is how you use the data you have collected, how it is summarized and presented.

Stage 3 – Evaluation

You must:
- Show active practical involvement over a period of time (the more active, the better!).
- Evaluate the good and bad points of the project, your Action Plan, the strategies used and the lessons learnt.
- Recognize your and others' views, experiences and contributions to the citizenship activity.
- Reflect on the value and success of the activity, the lessons you have learned/achieved and the benefit gained by others (say what changes you would suggest).

The key is evaluate what you did, what others did, what was achieved and what lessons were learned and what could have been improved.

Finally, remember the quality of written communication is also assessed, so redraft your report to write in a clear style, and check that spelling, punctuation and grammar are accurate.

Now it is Your Turn

In your groups, begin to discuss the ideas offered. Select one or two activities that interest you and think about the following points:

1 Give the activity a title and a very brief description of what it is and how it might develop.
2 Consider the resources you may need to get started.
3 How do you plan to use your time?
4 What personal skills will you need?
5 How will you gather the information you require?
6 How will you sort through the material and decide what is best to use in your final report?
7 What opinions and conclusions will you be able to draw from the activity?
8 How might it be improved?

Remember, as you write up your report it has to have a structure to gain marks. Your coursework is worth 40 per cent of the final mark!

---

i   INFO BOX

LAST MINUTE REMINDERS:
Remember you must:
- Plan.
- Give an account of your activity.
- Evaluate the activity.
- Produce a Resources List.

Glossary Index

Index